D0536879

you look tired

you look tired

AN EXCRUCIATINGLY HONEST
GUIDE TO NEW PARENTHOOD

jenny true

RUNNING PRESS

PHILADELPHIA

Running Press
Hachette Book Group
1290 Avenue of the Americas, New York, NY 10104
www.runningpress.com
@Running_Press

Printed in the United States of America

Published by Running Press, an imprint of Perseus Books, LLC, a subsidiary of Hachette Book Group, Inc. The Running Press name and logo is a trademark of the Hachette Book Group.

The Hachette Speakers Bureau provides a wide range of authors for speaking events. To find out more, go to www.hachettespeakersbureau.com or call (866) 376-6591

The publisher is not responsible for websites (or their content) that are not owned by the publisher.

Print book cover and interior design by Susan Van Horn

Library of Congress Control Number: 2020951564

ISBNs: 978-0-7624-7347-2 (hardcover) 978-0-7624-7350-2 (ebook)

LSC-C

Printing 1, 2021

**for all the pregnant people
and new parents**

"What if, instead of worrying about scaring pregnant women, people told them the truth?" —MEAGHAN O'CONNELL,
*And Now We Have Everything:
On Motherhood Before I Was Ready*

for copper

"Being your mother has required one act of vulgarity after another, and I am so strung out on you I couldn't care less." —CAMILLE T. DUNGY,
*Guidebook to Relative Strangers:
Journeys into Race, Motherhood, and History*

contents

I

WTF
I'M PREGNANT

"I'm going to be a good mom? What the fuck do they know? They don't know me!"

—KRISTEN, *mom of two*

1) **what moustache**
Pregnancy fucks with your body.

When I was five months pregnant, in an attempt to cheer myself up, I took myself out for a pedicure. This is how that went.

> **JENNY:** Hi! Do you have time for a pedicure?
> **TIFFANY** (peering at me): You want lip wax?
> **JENNY:** Ha, ha! Do I need it?
> **TIFFANY:** And chin wax?
> **JENNY:** WHAT THE FUCK ARE YOU TALKING ABOUT.

I have never been one for "taking care of my skin" or "doing my hair" or "brushing my teeth." But I will occasionally take myself out for some kind of treatment. I have had a couple of facials. I have sat in a mud bath. I once nearly fainted in a Russian wet sauna.

This is all to say that if you care about how you look or feel, pregnancy can be a challenging time.

*

I remember, ten or more years ago—before partner (hereafter known as Strong Jawline, or "SJ"), before child (hereafter known as Gargantu-baby, or "GB")—driving up Dolores Street in San Francisco in my manual Toyota Corolla and seeing a woman walking down the sidewalk on the other side of the street. I couldn't figure out what the fuck she was wearing. It was jeans, but at the top was . . . fabric? It was attached, but it looked like . . . a scarf? It was bunched, *ruched*, but it made no sense. Then it hit me: The woman was wearing *maternity pants*, but she wasn't pregnant. *She was wearing maternity pants as a fashion statement.*

I've lived in the San Francisco Bay Area since 1998, after four gray years in Evanston, Illinois. The temperate breezes and ocean air of San Francisco, discovered during a college internship, were a balm. So were the weirdos and freaks, the people who threw on living room curtains—or nothing at all!—and stalked out their front doors in the morning, ready to protest for peace in the Middle East or just ride around naked on a bicycle.

I moved as soon as I could after graduating, and for almost twenty years, I hopped from one crap apartment to the next, moving in and out of relationships and jobs, dating men and women, getting married, getting divorced, working as a freelance writer, a full-time editor, and a part-time babysitter.

Then, in my mid-thirties, I found myself single and living in a beautiful one-bedroom apartment across the San Francisco Bay in Deep East Oakland.

I had so much potential then. I had finally broken free of some horrible thoughts about myself and was making Good Choices. I was traveling to faraway places to learn about different cultures and peoples. I had fantastic neighbors and was involved in my community. I was gaining so much perspective and compassion for my fellow humans, understanding more deeply my privilege and my small place in the world.

Then I turned thirty-nine. I'd always been ambivalent about having kids, but I also thought they'd just sort of happen. They didn't! Cue biological clock ticking, and a brief spate of focused dating. Almost immediately, I met SJ, a beekeeper and a gardener. The next year, I was living in his house in San Francisco with our baby, two strollers, and an acute sense of whiplash.

*

For those people with access to prenatal care WHY IS THIS NOT EVERYONE, the no. 1 thing you need to understand about your pregnancy is this: Your ob-gyn might be a very nice person. They might have gone through childbirth personally, even multiple times. But their job—their priority—is not your comfort. It's your *safety*. Which means their mind is on worst-case scenarios (yours may be, too!). They will not be volunteering information about your pregnancy unless you show signs of something *serious*, such as:

1 Gestational diabetes

2 Hyperemesis gravidarum (extreme vomiting)

3 Preeclampsia (a potentially fatal condition)

4 A sudden need to wear patterns

So, the incredible truth is that there's no profession for guiding a person through the nearly yearlong process of being pregnant, even though our bodies will change in bewildering, yet predictable, ways as we gestate another human being. Besides doctors and nurses, professionals in the pregnancy/postpartum world focus on the birth part (midwives, doulas) or the part where your baby needs to eat (lactation consultants).

Who does that leave us with? The village. The problem? THE VILLAGE ISN'T TALKING.

(MAYBE THE VILLAGE IS BUSY RAISING KIDS AND GLAD THAT PREGNANCY IS IN THE REARVIEW MIRROR—BYE, FELICIA.)

Here is some basic information, which a professional, if there were one, would be able to help you anticipate and prepare for:

1 Your temperature will be permanently elevated. Like, you will have a fever for ten months.

2 Being pregnant feels like you're playacting pushing your stomach out, but you can't bring it back in.

3 If you didn't have a moustache already, you have one now. Also a beard.

4 Your nails and hair will grow faster than mold on a plastic-wrapped vegetable.

5 You will be hungry as fuck. Sore as fuck. Tired as fuck. Your boobs will ache. Your gums may bleed. Your skin may itch. You may get headaches. You may get acne. The skin around your eyes may swell. Your feet and ankles and hands may swell so much that you can't wear your shoes or gloves or rings. You may get cramps and stretch marks. You may get a linea nigra on your belly, and your nipples may darken. You may get melasma, or "the mask of pregnancy," on your face. You may get heartburn, and, toward the end, breathing may get harder and you will definitely need to pee thirty times a day.

There's more. SO MUCH MORE.

But here's something interesting: No one—not even the baby books—will tell you that some things get *better* when you get pregnant. You'd think since there's some good news, they'd be all over it, BUT NO.

Some examples:

1 **You stop getting your period!** Let's appreciate this for a moment. These are the things you don't need to buy or think about for ten months: tampons, panty liners, extra laundry soap for when you invariably bleed around the panty liner or just fucking forget today's the day, painkillers, and birth control.

2 **Some pains go away with pregnancy!** Both my shoulder impingement and metatarsalgia, a fancy word for YOUR FOOT HURTS WHEN YOU WALK ON IT, simply disappeared, possibly because of the same hormone-related loosening of ligaments that helps with birth.

3 SEX IS AMAZING. That pregnancy glow? Not a myth. During pregnancy, a whole bunch of blood settles in your nether regions and changes the fucking game. But it's specific to the second trimester, known to insiders (mostly partners) as the "party-mester." Pregnant people who can't stay awake for longer than a few hours at a time and are always sorta barfy? Not pregnancy glow. Pregnant people whose bodies are so distended that forward motion depends upon a sort of side-to-side waddle and who can't take the train all the way to work without stopping at Panera to pee? Not pregnancy glow.

But: Pregnant people whose hair is suddenly full, whose baby bump is obvious but not yet ponderous, whose breasts are round and high,* who (for the most part) are past the barfiness and compulsive sleeping and who (for the most part) experience a completely bizarre, given the circumstances, boost of energy?

Watch out for these people, because they are *fucking*.

I'm not sure why no one told me, since I have a bit of a reputation as being the Most Likely to Talk about Sex When No One Else Really Wants To. I have always felt, perhaps wrongly, that people want to hear about my sexcapades. When I was eight, I tried to teach a neighbor girl how to masturbate (forever after, when I walked over to her house to play, she told me through the screen door that she was "busy." Another eight-year-old. "Busy."). I tried to masturbate under my desk in my sixth-grade science class. I have had orgasms in my sleep. I have had sex in abandoned buildings, cars, offices, boats, hot tubs, pools, tents, hotel rooms, hostels, conference rooms, bathrooms, cabanas, an olive orchard, the woods, the beach, a church, and a duck pond (well, *near* a duck pond). I kept a travel blog listing all the places I'd had sex, which included the Andaman Sea, Norway, China, Laos, Belize, Thailand,

---

*One thing that grieved me during my pregnancy was that, as my boobs got bigger, the small one didn't look any less like a tortilla chip taped to my chest. It didn't get any *rounder*. It just looked like a bigger tortilla chip.

Bali, Venezuela, Vietnam, Iceland, Italy, Sicily, Germany, Cambodia, Chile, and England—and look, I'm listing them again!

Still, I was unprepared for the miracle that is pregnancy sex.

SJ has a handheld shower nozzle in his house (now my house). I thought I noticed early on in my pregnancy that when I used it to wash my stuff, I was hypersensitive. But I never brought this up to my ob-gyn, because she hadn't brought it up to me. No one ever told me I wasn't imagining things, and this is what makes me BANANACAKES. WHY NOT JUST TELL PEOPLE THAT, WHEN YOU GET PREGNANT, MORE BLOOD GOES TO YOUR GENI-TAL AREA, MAKING EVERYTHING MORE SENSITIVE.

That groan-y shower experience had a flip side: I could not get enough sex! SJ still talks about a weekend trip we took during the party-mester. We had sex eight times in twenty-four hours in a bed-and-breakfast near a trickling stream. He's still sore—but I'm pretty sure if I suggested another trip, he'd finish his game of Grand Theft Auto, eat a fried chicken sand-wich, throw his toothbrush in his pocket, and meet me in the van.

Unfortunately, pregnancy sex doesn't last. My friend Cati told me, "The sex now is good. It's *great*. But it will never be the same as when I was pregnant."

Then she cried.

JENNY TRUE'S REASONS NOT TO GET PREGNANT

❶ It's really uncomfortable for a long time.

❷ No one will help you.

JENNY TRUE'S REASONS TO GET PREGNANT

❶ Baby.

❷ Pregnancy sex.

---

2) people will touch you
You think they won't. But they will!

Someone I didn't know touched my belly when I was pregnant.

I had nearly made it—I was in my third trimester, and no one had touched me yet. Little did I know, the third trimester is prime time for Oh Hell No Stranger.

One day I walked outside to get something from my car, and right in front of my house, two women I had never seen, one curiously sedate and carrying a small dog and the other with a slightly frenzied vibe, stopped in their tracks.

By this time I was in the Regal Phase of pregnancy: moving slow, slitted eyes, posture wrenched up and back. Taking up a lot of room. I hadn't smiled in weeks. I did not look like someone you would reach out and rub.

But these women were overcome with emotion at the sight of me. Notes:

1 Slipping away from people becomes impossible when you're pregnant. Pregnant people do not "slip." They "lurch," "barrel," or "trudge." Strangers without Boundaries become your cross to bear.

2 The Regal Phase is not only physical but mental. I had become an excellent listener (or skilled at *appearing* to listen, while my endless to-do-before-baby-arrives list flipped forward in my brain like an old-timey train station timetable). I became a nodder. Patient. I mean, when everyone temporarily treats you like a fucking oracle, you take on the mantle. Plus, absolutely nothing going on in the world farther than a foot away could sustain my interest. My circle, already, had become very small.

And these women were inside my circle.

"You . . . ," said Slightly Frenzied.

"Me," I said.

"You're pregnant!" she said.

"I am!" I said.

"It's such a beautiful time," she gabbled. "I mean, I've never been pregnant. Neither has she."

Small Dog shook her head. The small dog sniffed.

The sun was shining, and I wasn't at work, so I was in a great mood. I remember checking in with myself to see whether I minded being accosted, and I didn't, because through her scrim of frenzied energy, the woman chattering away seemed, in her bumbling way, genuine.

So when she reached across the divide that normally separates two strangers and rubbed my belly—then chattered some more, then did it again—I didn't punch her. I just felt surprised it hadn't happened already, since Strangers without Boundaries are kind of a thing in the United States (see: White women touching Black women's hair, anti-choice legislation, etc.).

It was a reminder that women's bodies do not belong to us, and *pregnant* people's bodies belong to everyone.

Here's the thing: You are allowed to do whatever you want with your pregnant body. You can invite people to touch it. You can invite people to feel the baby kick, and, in fact, this is encouraged with partners, who need to understand the constant nature of Being Pregnant and especially Being Very Pregnant and who can't feel the baby turning, hiccupping, pressing against your butthole, or trying to punch its way outside.

But Other People are not allowed to touch you without asking first. And people who ask need to be ready to hear no.

In this situation, I didn't mind being touched. I'm not the kind of person—middle-aged-ish, White, of average to less-than-average beauty—who ever draws attention, so being noticed was a novelty. But for those who would rather not be touched, here is some advice:

THE JENNY TRUE GUIDE TO WHAT TO DO IF SOME JERK TRIES TO TOUCH YOUR PREGNANT BELLY WITHOUT YOUR PERMISSION

1 Shout, "BEEP! BEEP!," and back up, like a truck.

2 Scream like a rabbit:

> **SJ** (to our son): Do you know what sound a bunny makes?
>
> **GARGANTUBABY:** (No answer, because what sound does a bunny make?)
>
> **SJ:** (Puts on GB's bunny ears, throws back his head, and makes a screaming sound)
>
> **JENNY:** Is that the sound a bunny makes?
>
> **SJ:** Yeah, if you put it in a cage with a snake.

3 *From my friend Jill:* We are days away from baby. I am in line at a restaurant and a thirtysomething woman turns around, sees my bump, and ***REACHES OUT AND TOUCHES MY STOMACH.***

> **HER:** How cute!
>
> **ME:** (firmly) Please don't touch me. You really need to ask.
>
> THE WOMAN LOOKS UTTERLY SHOCKED.
>
> **HER:** You don't need to be a bitch about it.
>
> !?!?!?!!
>
> **ME:** Fuck off. I'm putting a curse on your dog. (I stare at her dog.) (I'm not a fan of dogs inside restaurants.)

The end.

3) it was never about you

Waiters who take away the wine-glasses, and medical personnel who refer to you as "Mom."

One day on Facebook—NOTHING GOOD EVER COMES FROM THAT OPENER—I read a post from a colleague, someone I admire and who helped me early in my career. I'll call him Gay White Man. He complained, among other things, about women with children and pregnant people going to the front of bathroom lines. Then he wrote angrily, "Having kids is a choice."

OH MY GOD. This is someone who is CLOSE WITH HIS MOTHER.

The trip about being pregnant for the first time is that your personal world—the way you see it, the way you see yourself in it—shifts in a unique way, at the same time that you're having the most universal of experiences.

Let me clear something up: No one else thinks you're having a unique experience. You are simply fulfilling your corporal duty as one of the Baby Makers of Planet Earth.

GWM has allies in his indignation at the idea that pregnant people and new parents get "special treatment," including the US government: Pregnancy is so expected, so taken for granted, that in the United States, *some* workers—but not all—get twelve weeks of *unpaid* leave after they have a baby.

The message? FIGURE IT OUT. YOU'RE THE IDIOT WHO GOT PREGNANT.

Pregnancy is when you find out that the goiter you've been gestating and that's so important to you is revered in theory but scorned in practice. Also, it has reduced you to a word: *Mom*. It's a little confusing, because you thought *Mom* was a term of respect, but it doesn't feel respectful when other people say it because, you know, you have a fucking name.

I ran into this during childbirth. My labor was long. From the time my water broke to the time Gargantubaby's slick, hairy head emerged from my swollen vagina, forty hours had passed. I spent sixteen of those hours in a hospital.

After I'd begged for an epidural (peace out, natural birth plan!) and spent the next ten hours in a bed numb below the waist, one of the nurses said it was time to push.

"You'll have to show me how, because I can't feel anything," I said.

"We'll practice," she assured me.

"About how long does this part take?" I was exhausted but still high, after ten hours of an epidural, on not feeling pain anymore as I just lay around waiting for my son to appear. The nurse, Jackie, smiled.

"You know there's no way to tell?" she said.

"Ballpark."

"Sometimes it takes two hours, sometimes four. I don't want to promise anything."

"Average?"

"Two hours."

Jackie and another nurse put my legs up in stirrups. SJ held back one of my legs, and the doula I was privileged to hire held the other. I was really worried about my right leg falling off and breaking because I couldn't feel it AT ALL. Jackie said that when she gave me the go-ahead, I would hold the backs of my thighs, pull myself up slightly, take a deep breath, and "push" as we counted to ten. She stood at the end of the bed between my legs and watched the monitor over my right shoulder. When the monitor indicated a contraction had started, she nodded and said, "OK, push for ten seconds." I squeezed, hoping this was "pushing," and watched Jackie's eyes go wide. She put her hand between my legs.

"What's happening?" I said.

"He's coming!" she said.

"THANK YOU, JESUS," I said.

She literally held my son inside me with her fingertips as the midwife and some other nurses rushed into the room. And that is how, after sixteen hours of being in the hospital, I met the woman who delivered my baby.

I liked the midwife. She had curly hair, and she was funny, which is pretty much all I require of a person. But during the birth, she called me "Mom," as in, "OK, Mom, when I say push, you push." And I remember thinking, I know we just met since you only roll in for this part and you do this all day, every day, but isn't my name on some kind of chart?

Then, a year and a half after my son was born, I had surgery on my ovary.

One Friday, I was misdiagnosed with ovarian cancer. SUCH A FUN WEEKEND.

"You have a mass," the doctor said, rolling back from the exam table. "It's about this size." She cupped her fingers and pantomimed an apple.

Then she left the room for a week to order an ultrasound and I went somewhere else as I stared out the windows. When she came back, I said, "Can you repeat everything you said before?"

She did, with a couple changes and additions.

"So you don't think it's a cyst. You think it's a tumor," I said.

"Yes," she said. "I've had cancer, so I'm going to treat it that way until I know otherwise."

SJ and I spent the weekend vacillating between morbid jokes and total silence. I tried to act normal around GB as he gaped, awestruck, at the ducks in Golden Gate Park. On Monday, I learned that what I had was a *benign* tumor, something disgusting called a dermoid cyst, that needed to be removed.

Two and a half months later, I had surgery. It did not go as planned, since the cyst ruptured as the surgeons were trying to take it out. After a few days at home, I was so out of my mind with pain and disorientation that the recovery was not going the way I'd been told it would that I had a panic attack, and I insisted that SJ call 911. Even as I crouched, hyperventilating, on the living room floor, convinced that I was dying, I called out directions to put the dog in a bedroom, since I'd read this is the polite thing to do when one is expecting firefighters or EMTs.

The two kind souls who trooped into my house, surreptitiously counted my pain pills, held my hand, and led me through breathing exercises addressed me as "Mom," which I found odd, because when they asked me my name, that wasn't what I said.

So the odd thing about being pregnant (and a new parent) is that you feel like the center of attention, but you soon realize that no one cares enough to learn your name. For example, an abundance of attention is paid to your *body* when you're pregnant. You get a barrage of information about how to avoid harming the fetus—no unpasteurized cheese, no raw meat or fish, no cocaine, only medications that are approved by your doctor. This attention COMPLETELY FUCKS OFF once the baby is not in your body anymore. The BABY continues to get regular checkups until age two, but you get one or two until six weeks after the baby is born. Then you disappear from everyone's radar, and you are no longer you. You are "Mom."

Some of us don't hate being called "Mom." Some of us have been waiting to get pregnant a really fucking long time, and the more people who call us "Mom," the more the universe will ensure that we bring this baby safely to term. Also, it's like a primer, practicing for being someone's parent and getting used to the idea (although my son is three, and I'm still not used to the idea. Why does he cry when I leave the room? He wants me? Why?).

If you're new to the practice of being called "Mom" rather than your own fucking name, especially when you're going through childbirth and panic attacks, here's some guidance:

THE JENNY TRUE NAMING ACTIVITY

1 Do you mind being called "Mom" by people who are not your child?

   ○ *No. (Go to chapter 4.)*

   ○ *Yes. (Go to question 2.)*

2 What was your nickname as a kid?

_____

3 Would you like this to be your nickname now?

   ○ *No. (Go to question 4.)*

   ○ *Yes. (Go to chapter 4.)*

4 What are some of your most distinctive qualities? Select all that apply.

○ *Curiosity*

○ *Kindness*

○ *Patience*

○ *Rage*

○ *Malapropisms*

○ *Passive-aggression*

○ *Botched apologies*

○ *Blurting something out before thinking of a better way to say it*

○ *Copying people on emails who don't really need to be copied so everyone will know your righteousness*

○ *Spitting out food if you're not really enjoying it*

○ *Hugging other people when you're aware that you're sweating*

5 Choose one quality from those you checked in question 4. Now, do any of the following titles apply to you?

> *Ms.*
> *Mr.*
> *Mx.*
> *Miss*
> *Mrs.*
> *Dr.*
> *Nope.*

6 Choose one title from question 5, or none. Combine it with your choice from question 4. Write it below:

_____

7 Do you prefer being referred to as your answer to question 6, or "Mom"?

○ *It doesn't matter. This whole exercise has been a waste of your time. You're "Mom" now!*

4) you have no fucking idea what this feels like

Useful ways to communicate that pregnancy is a challenging time.

I fell on my ass a week after finding out I was pregnant. It was November in Oakland, California. The air was humid but cool. The five-year drought that had broken in March had given way to occasional torrential rains. My apartment was full of unopened wine and champagne bottles from my fortieth birthday party the week before, a daylong open house for which my parents had flown in from Illinois, my father had made his famous hummus, and sixty friends, neighbors, and coworkers—including SJ, who arrived with his then-six-year-old daughter and a beautiful necklace—drove in from around the Bay Area and plied me with coconut cake, cards, and gifts.

At twilight that morning, on my way to the bathroom, I fell down the split-level stairs between the bedroom and the tile floor of the entryway. I had NEVER fallen down ANY stairs, and I have been severely nearsighted since the second grade, so I was well-versed both in putting on my glasses when I got up from bed and holding on to the banister on my way to this particular toilet—neither of which I did this time, and I was wearing socks, so I slipped on my heels.

As I lay on the steps, my lower back pulsing from where I'd landed on it, I thought, *People do this on purpose to end pregnancies. No one will believe this was an accident.*

SJ lived somewhere amid the twinkling lights across the bay I could see through the living room windows. So there was no one around to cry to or yell at. I had to get my pregnant ass up on my own, drag myself to the toilet, and sit there thinking about all the sudden, bewildering changes in my life.

Some pregnant people have partners. You know, the people who "stand by our sides" as we morph into balloon animals and whose job, we are told, is to take care of us so we can take care of the baby.

USELESS.

Most of these people have never been pregnant (although some desperately want to be—my friend Chrissy says that after her wife gave birth to their daughter, she "tried to give birth to our second kid, and it didn't happen, so in some circles I am a failed, barren non-birthing parent"). These people have only a voyeur's understanding of what it's like. They furrow their brows in sympathy, nod, hold our hands, wipe our tears and snotty noses with their shirts.

USELESS.

Our jobs? We're told it's to "rest," "take care of ourselves" (WE'LL GET TO MY THOUGHTS ON SELF-CARE IN CHAPTER 29), eat healthy foods, take prenatal vitamins, get exercise, and generally protect this shining vessel no one cared about before.

But that's not our only job. We have another, equally important job, and that is to inform our partners (if we have them) of how they will never, ever understand the extent of our discomfort and pain or be able to pay us back.

This is what SJ did for me while I was pregnant:

1. **Rebuilt his kitchen, by hand, with supplies from IKEA.**

2. **Dismantled his old, out-of-tune piano, by hand, and dragged it to the driveway for a bulky-items pickup because I didn't want it.**

3. **Put me on the deed to his house.**

USELESS.

One afternoon, months after I'd moved into his house with my cream, single-cushion Crate & Barrel couch and an Arco knockoff floor lamp (and carted half of SJ's Hawaiian shirts to Goodwill but left his wall-size poster of *Blade Runner* and his animal skull collection), I crawled into bed at 3:30 p.m. and didn't get out again until 8 p.m. I was thirty-eight weeks pregnant. It had not been a good week. I had succumbed to parental leave, but I had acid reflux and cramping that kept me up at night, and I'd attended my final pre-baby class, infant and child CPR and choking, in which I got to fantasize *while holding a doll* about worst-case scenarios when I hadn't even met my kid yet.

I'd made a list of things that had become difficult:

1 Putting my shoes on.

2 Sitting for any length of time.

3 Standing for any length of time.

4 Giving two fucks about your bullshit.

That evening, desperate to finish the to-do items on a different list, I sat in bed researching pediatricians. SJ came home and poked his head into the room, looking pleased with himself.

SJ: Guess what I did today!
JENNY: Did you research pediatricians, too? Did you set up the diaper sprayer on the toilet tank? Did you put together the stroller?
SJ (HOLDING UP SOMETHING): I got us a pizza cutter!

Some baby books will try to tell you that partners are "going through something, too," something that gets overlooked with all the attention on the pregnant person (or, as the pregnant person will clarify, the attention on the fetus).

WHO CARES.

These people need to start training *before* you get pregnant for their *real* job: FAILING.

With that in mind, here are the most effective techniques for getting across your discomfort, pain, exhaustion, anxiety, exhaustion, constipation, exhaustion, and exhaustion.

THE JENNY TRUE GUIDE TO INVOLVING YOUR PARTNER, IF YOU HAVE ONE, IN YOUR PREGNANCY

1 **Ask trick questions.** For example, "What did *you* do today?," "Oh, you slept well last night?," and "So you've been 'preparing' for the baby?"

2 **Make demands for sex.** Use neutral language: "I won't cry this time" or "I won't throw up this time."

3 **Make impossible requests.** For example, "Will you please just set up the crib so the baby gets sun on her face but not in her eyes?"

4 **When all else fails, have a fight in the car:**

SJ: I have to tell you, I'm really upset about something.

JENNY: What are you upset about?

SJ: You did this thing that really upset me, and we've talked about it before, so I don't know why you did it again.

JENNY: (Stares out the window silently, imagining withdrawing all the money I brought into our marriage and that is still legally mine and then, I don't know, escaping somewhere so I don't have to deal with other human beings and a never-ending to-do list.)

SJ: What's going on over there?

JENNY: This is my version of what happened, and, yes, maybe I shouldn't have done that, but what else was I supposed to do?

SJ: You could have done this thing we talked about before.

JENNY: HERE'S A BETTER IDEA: WHY DON'T YOU SHOVE IT. AND NOT TO CHANGE THE SUBJECT BUT YOUR RESPONSE TO THIS PLAYS ON MY VULNERABILITIES ABOUT NEEDING TO TRUST AND RELY ON ANOTHER PERSON WHEN THAT MUTUALITY HASN'T EXACTLY WORKED OUT FOR ME IN THE PAST.

SJ: THAT MIGHT BE WHAT YOU'RE THINKING, BUT THAT'S NOT WHAT YOU'RE SAYING SO NOW I'M RESPONDING TO WHAT YOU'RE SAYING.

JENNY: (SAYS SOMETHING WITH THE WORD *FUCKING* IN IT.)

SJ: (SAYS SOMETHING WITH THE WORD *FUCKING* IN IT.)

JENNY: (STARTS MAKING A LIST OF EVERYTHING I'VE SAC-RIFICED TO MAKE THIS WORK AND THEN DEMANDS TO KNOW WHAT SJ HAS SACRIFICED.)

SJ: (ATTEMPTS TO TELL ME WHAT HE'S SACRIFICED.)

JENNY: (INTERRUPTS AND DISAGREES THAT THESE THINGS CONSTITUTE SACRIFICES IN ANY WAY COMPARABLE TO WHAT I HAVE SACRIFICED.)

Later that same night, SJ made me chocolate-chip cookies.

JENNY: You are a fucking champ.

SJ: (Smiles)

JENNY: Did you think that's how that sentence was going to end?

SJ: I was keeping an open mind.

5) people have opinions

You're doing everything wrong.

You might think that pregnancy is a time to reflect—on the meaning of life, on our purpose in the world—and to prepare—for our worlds to change, for our hearts to grow. It may seem like a real coming together of the past and the future, with pregnancy the limbo.

The rest of the world sees it as a time for us to prove how stupid we are.

The list of things you can do wrong starts rattling by in a continuous loop the second you become pregnant, because you might not have used the best, most accurate pregnancy test (are you even pregnant?). You might not have signed on with the greatest ob-gyn, and there are things you need, and you should get them, now.

There's your health to consider, and the health of the baby. Are you taking fish oil? Which brand? Liquid or capsule? You have your prenatal vitamins, right? What about exercise? Are you doing enough to help the baby, but not so much that you'd hurt the baby?

You definitely need a bassinet, but not that bassinet, and you need a newborn stroller and an umbrella stroller and a jogger and, oh, you don't jog? Do you hate yourself?

You need a nursery, like an extra room in your home, and you don't have an extra room? Hmm. Can you relocate? Because the baby needs to sleep in a crib in a separate room, but you also need to co-sleep because your baby won't love you if you don't.

You need to start thinking about whether you're going to breast-feed, because breast is best, although fed is best (although breast is best) (although fed is best), and you'll need to buy nursing bras and outrageously expensive cover-ups because, although breast is best (although fed is best), titties are shameful and breastfeeding is disgusting and no one wants to see that and you'll need breast milk bags and a pump and all the pump parts, because even though you're going to breastfeed (because breast is best) (although fed is best) you need to make MORE milk between feedings in case you don't make enough overall, but we don't know how much your baby is going to need and we don't know how much your body is going to make or whether it's going to make any at all, which, if it doesn't, will be your failure as a woman, and your baby may not latch, which will also be your fault.

You need bottles. Glass is best but be careful because glass breaks, and plastic can work but remember about the BPAs and DEFINITELY don't warm up milk in the microwave, and did you know you need different size bottles for different stages? I mean, you can't use an eight-ounce bottle with a newborn or a four-ounce bottle with a six-month-old. You need them all, all the bottles, because you can buy them in two-ounce, five-ounce, nine-ounce, and eleven-ounce, and you need all the bottle parts, the nipples and rings and covers and valves and vents and brushes to clean them and a cute dish rack for bottle parts and you need a bag to carry the bottles and an ice pack to keep the milk cold. But not too cold. Because babies don't drink milk cold; they like their milk warm! Duh!

Swaddles are important. You need to know how to swaddle. Take all the blankets from the hospital, but also muslin works, and now they have these swaddles with Velcro so you don't really need to know how to swaddle. Unless you don't get the swaddles with Velcro, and then you need to know how to swaddle.

Infant CPR. It doesn't matter if the image of an infant needing CPR sends you into a spiral of grief and panic. You need to go to a class, you need to watch, you need to learn, you need to practice, you need to pump the heels of your hands on the lower half of a doll's sternum to the tune of "Stayin' Alive," doing thirty compressions at the rate of twice a second, and then tip up the doll's head, pinch the nose shut, cover the mouth with yours, and give two breaths, and then when the rules change months later to something called "hands-only CPR," keep the fuck up.

You definitely need to carry your baby, and we have invented a term to describe this, *baby wearing*, which just means carrying your baby, which you have to do anyway to get it from point A to point B. But just in case you were thinking of putting your baby in a stroller, which you need (see above), or carrying the baby so it is *not* squished against your sweaty, hormone-seeping skin like a starfish BUT FOR GOD'S SAKE LEAVING THE AIRWAY UNBLOCKED, don't. Carry it. I mean, wear it. I mean, baby wearing is the same as carrying your baby, but you have to carry your baby the *right* way, and you have to carry it the right way *all the time*, or it doesn't count as baby wearing, and baby wearing is the only way to connect with your baby, and if you don't do it the right way, your baby won't love you, and also we will come after you.

You might want to start thinking about your baby's skin. You'll need hypoallergenic shampoo and soap, but really, you don't need to use shampoo or soap on your newborn at all, just water will work. And definitely get hypoallergenic laundry detergent, and wash everything all the time, but you don't really need to wash everything all the time because it's a baby, but if there's even the slightest bit of poop on something you'll want to wash that. And buy organic cotton, even though it's scratchier than any other fabric and four times as expensive, but buy the softest clothing to protect your baby's skin, and buy nothing that's flame-retardant because your baby will breathe in the chemicals that make it flame-retardant, but if you don't buy clothes that are flame-retardant they'll be the first thing to go in a house fire.

Hello?

Hello?

6) **birth hurts**
Prenatal yoga is a waste of time.

Before giving birth, I confided to SJ that no matter how many birth stories I heard—Asked for! Begged for!—I told myself, "They're exaggerating." I didn't really believe it. I didn't! How bad could it be?

One coworker said she'd birthed an eight-pound baby with a head circumference in the ninety-ninth percentile. Another said her baby came out with her elbow crooked above her head, like a superhero shooting razors out of her tricep.

Whatever. So many people I knew had gone through childbirth and seemed fine. My own mother said both of her labors had been three hours and that they felt like "crampy stuff":

ROSE: I didn't really feel you kick until the end.

JENNY: What do you mean, *the end*?

ROSE: Well, the last eight or nine months.

JENNY: Mom, the whole pregnancy is eight or nine months.

ROSE: So the end. Like the last couple months.

JENNY: You didn't feel me at all until the last couple months?

ROSE: No.

JENNY: You keep telling me these things about your pregnancies that are not normal at all. I think you're just not remembering.

ROSE (laughs): Maybe.

OH MY GOD CHILDBIRTH HURTS. I HAVE NEVER FELT SUCH PAIN IN MY LIFE AND ANYONE WHO TELLS YOU IT'S "EXTREMELY UNCOMFORTABLE" OR FEELS LIKE "CRAMPY STUFF" (MOM) IS LYING.

You'd think I would have believed that birth hurts, because while you're pregnant, all the people who have gone before will rally to tell you how their babies ripped apart their vaginas.

These same people will try to get you to go to a prenatal yoga class, telling you it makes things better. Names will be passed around, studios recommended. Someone may want you to go to a class so fucking bad they'll buy you a gift card.

Someone bought me a gift card, so I went. But the first time I went I was so early along I didn't show, and I felt like a big faker. I walked into a room full of pregnant people in their third trimesters—the experts, the almost-theres—and instantly felt out of my league. They were fucking gorgeous: round everywhere, huge hair, pedicures, feather earrings. I was pale and barfy and almost apologized for being there when we went around the room for introductions. (Anytime you go to a meeting of pregnant people, you will share your name and the single thing about you that matters: how many weeks you are. People in their first trimester are not permitted to make eye contact with people in their third trimester.)

It was only when I got to my third trimester that I understood. It's important to note that I didn't look gorgeous in my third trimester. I have pictures from my baby shower I would rather not look at: choppy haircut, too much makeup, pale, lumpy (although I was happy—somebody let me drink a mimosa). But whether you're gorgeous or just fucking not (according to an internet algorithm, the celebrity I most resemble is Peter Sellers), when you get to your third trimester, you're OVER IT. And OVER IT is the root of cool.

Prenatal yoga is not just yoga with modifications for pregnant people. You go to a regular class for that and sit out half of it, which you always wanted to do but now you have an excuse. Prenatal yoga sells you a bill of goods: that if you practice certain poses and chant certain things, it will make the birth easier. It will encourage your baby to go doooooooown the birth canal. It will distract you from the pain. And, if you practice certain poses that are painful, such as squatting on the balls of your feet, you will better be able to withstand the pain of a contraction.

HORSESHIT. NOTHING CAN PREPARE YOU FOR THE PAIN OF A CONTRACTION, EVEN LESS FOR FORTY HOURS OF CONTRACTIONS.

Childbirth can be especially fraught for Black and Indigenous birthing people. Here's what that can look like:

Black or Indigenous birthing person: Something's wrong.

Nurse/Doctor: (Withholds information; Fails to communicate with team members; Introduces unnecessary interventions; Ignores; Reassures without checking symptoms because of ingrained belief that Black people have a higher pain threshold/don't understand their own bodies/ are at fault for preexisting health conditions)

Black or Indigenous birthing person and/or Black or Indigenous newborn: (Dies of something preventable)

Here are some additional activities people will tell you alleviate the pain of childbirth: relaxation, distraction, hypnosis, massage, therapeutic touch, movement, water.

LIES.

You know what helps? An epidural, and not having a baby.

There is no point in doing anything to prepare for childbirth. I say this as someone who did everything because I thought I could out-plan childbirth. I went to prenatal yoga. I took *SJ* to prenatal yoga and made him practice techniques at home. I read Ina May Gaskin. I meditated. I listened to meditation tapes.

> ROSE: I told somebody, "My daughter's trying to make the birth the best experience possible." (Then she laughed so hard she had to wipe her eyes.)

If relaxation tapes, meditation, and yoga help with your anxiety about how bad childbirth is going to hurt, go for it. But if the reason you're doing these activities is you have some idea that you're "preparing" for childbirth, reality check: Childbirth is shitty. Then it's over.

(Then there are afterpains.)

Here are some better ways to pass the time between getting pregnant and giving birth:

1. Learn the ukulele.
2. Play flashlight tag.
3. Join a choir.
4. Start an herb garden.
5. Volunteer at a monkey preserve.

6. Play Yahtzee.
7. Make a birdhouse.
8. Knit.
9. Felt.
10. Nap.

THE JENNY TRUE GUIDE TO PREPARING FOR CHILDBIRTH

① **Denial.** During the initial phase of pregnancy, when childbirth is so far away it doesn't seem possible, pretend it doesn't exist. Concentrate on not barfing and getting in twelve hours of sleep a day.

② **Panic.** As the fetus and the placenta grow larger and you start to understand that there are only a couple ways for them to come out, allow yourself to lie on your floor a little each day, paralyzed by terror.

③ **Anxiety.** Once the panic has subsided, let your fears settle into a constant, low-grade dread. This can manifest in planning and researching everything that has to do with pregnancy, childbirth, the postpartum phase, and parenting. The internet will provide.

④ **Denial.** Get your nails done.

⑤ **Denial.** Prenatal yoga.

"Elizabeth was a peaceful home birth. A water birth at my apartment. Picture-perfect. Except the back labor, which I described as normal birthing pains with André the Giant standing on your sacrum." —**DIANE**, *mom of two*

7) **birthing videos and baby advice books**
What to expect.

When I was pregnant, I took one look at a gift copy of *What to Expect When You're Expecting* and threw it into a garbage can in a parking garage. According to that book, one drop of alcohol will kill your baby, and if you're forty (which I was) your pregnancy is inherently high-risk, no matter your personal health history FEAR FEAR FEAR. It also conflates "becoming a mother" with "housework" and assumes we all had an "immaculate house" to begin with and that our values begin and end with keeping it that way.

Let's just say it wasn't for me.

When you're pregnant, baby advice books can be *wonderful*. I read them all, pregnancy and parenting books alike. I even spent some time with the classic *The Baby Book* by William and Martha Sears, a married couple who had ten kids and then had the audacity to write a book giving other people advice.

Pregnant people read these books because we're dying for insight on what's happening in our bodies. We're *excited*—we're about to have a baby! The most mind-blowing science fiction is happening right beneath our skin. Being pregnant is like binge-watching a really good TV show that never, ever gives up the goods. Each night we go to bed is a cliffhanger, and all we want is to race through the next three hundred episodes so we can SEE WHAT HAPPENS ALREADY. And we want to know how to do things right—how to take care of ourselves and the baby so everything will be perfect.

The problem is, there's no shortage of people willing to step in and tell us how.

I could rip on *What to Expect* all day (and I have!). But the problem is not with that book in particular: It's with the inherent negligence of writing a book that's ostensibly for all pregnant people and new parents, when our situations are vastly different. Case in point: How many books recommend that you just hire someone to clean your house before baby comes? This bit of advice is a staple in new-parent books, yet one in eight adults in the United States lives below the federal poverty line. So most of us are not hiring anybody to do some shit we could do ourselves.

One salve for baby books, though, is birthing videos. BIRTHING VIDEOS OMG.

Early on in my pregnancy, a friend sent me a link to a birthing video. I sat on the bed one afternoon with all my chins and my tissues, emotions at a hair trigger, and watched this person give birth over and over. I sobbed every time the baby came out, tiny and vulnerable and covered in white stuff, tiny fists balled at its cheeks, crying for its mother. That would be me! One day soon I would meet my child!

I sought out more videos. All the pregnant people in them were beautiful, wearing nice bras and, incredibly, jewelry IT'S A THING. I watched these people give birth in tubs and on beds and in cabins and cried and cried and cried.

For a time, inspired by these videos and afraid of a cascade of interventions at a hospital, I wanted a home birth. I kept the dream alive for months. I talked about it with SJ, who nodded and smiled, then went back to getting stung by his bees and turning his compost pile with a pitchfork.

One evening, we went to a meetup at a local birthing center. Bless their rich hearts—they charged EIGHT THOUSAND DOLLARS, none of which was covered by my insurance. We sat in a circle with the other couples, free snacks before us on a table. SJ and I were the oldest people by ten years, and every other pregnant person in the room was SEVEN TO EIGHT WEEKS PREGNANT. NOT EXAGGERATING. I KNOW BECAUSE WE WENT AROUND THE ROOM TO SHARE HOW MANY WEEKS WE WERE. They weren't out of miscarriage territory and they were interviewing midwives! Who were these organized bitches? And how could they afford $8,000? I took two mozzarella sticks, SJ pillaged the salted nuts, we dominated the Q&A, and we left without leaving a phone number.

My friend Diane had signed up with a birthing center, but nearly had her son in the car on the way there. "I almost had him on a busy street," she says, "where I opened up the car door to puke at a stoplight."

She made it to the center, but her labor happened so quickly she never made it into the tub. Also, the fact that 15 percent of planned home births end up happening in a hospital anyway made me look at other options. Finally, the fact that I'm basically risk-averse and my living room carpet is eighteen years old and I don't want to sit on it on a good day made the decision for me. Plus, the money: I settled on my employer-sponsored health care, which charged $200 a day, everything included. Sold!

So that was me, giving birth in a hospital with the doula I was privileged to hire spraying me with a shower nozzle and listening to me scream, "I WANT AN EPIDURAL," and murmuring, "But you wanted a natural birth," and grimacing as I screamed, "I'M NOT THAT PERSON."

When my son was born, I cried because I thought I was supposed to. People cried in the videos when they had babies. I *could* cry, because I was exhausted after forty hours, but mostly I cried because I had wired my brain, through multiple viewings of birth videos, to believe that I needed to have a video-ready EXPERIENCE. And crying was part of it.

The truth is I don't remember the second-by-second experience of my son's birth, because I was looped, having been awake and in a shocking amount of pain for thirty hours, then immobilized by an epidural for the next ten but still awake and numb below the waist. Also, when my son emerged, although my brain was taken over by the desperate need to protect him, I didn't know who he *was*. It was a very confusing forty hours.

Still, I squeezed out a few ugly tears, and we got it on camera.

THE JENNY TRUE GUIDE TO BOOKS NOT TO READ WHILE YOU'RE PREGNANT LEARN FROM ME

1 *Revenge*, by Jim Harrison

2 *Angels*, by Denis Johnson

3 *What to Expect When You're Expecting*, any edition

Pregnant people and new parents have various levels of tolerance for baby advice books. Here's what a few friends had to say:

"Grab a child development book before you grab a parenting book."

—DONNIE, *dad of one*

"Our pregnancy guide had all kinds of shit about making sure to get your toenails done before giving birth and how useless men are, so that just made us laugh and laugh and then angry."

—CHRISSY (AND SASHA), *moms of one*

"I heavily prepared for pregnancy and having a brand-new baby with books, classes, and even a birth retreat."

—KRISTEN, *mom of two*

"Our adoption agency required us to take two daylong parenting-preparation classes, after which I thought, 'Why don't bio parents have to take classes? These are really helpful!'"

—ANN, *mom of two*

"I devoured baby books. Read at least three of them, obsessing on the symptoms of each trimester to the kind of detergent to buy."

—STEPHANIE, *mom of one*

"My experience with parenting books is that I will buy a parenting book on the recommendation of a parent friend, and then put it, unread, on the parenting bookshelf, where it will no doubt stay unread until the children move out."

—LORI, *mom of two*

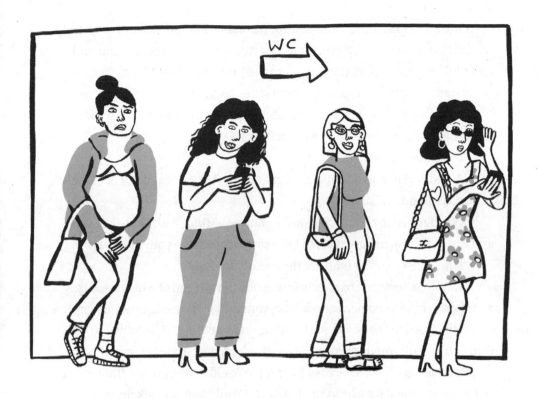

8) the line for the bathroom

Out of my way, fuckers!

By the time I was in my third trimester, I knew the bathroom code at the Panera between my home and my job, since I could not make the forty-five-minute commute, which comprised a half-hour train ride and fifteen minutes of walking, without stopping to pee.

Once, I skipped the Panera stop, believing I could make it WORST DECISION THAT DAY. By the time I started the walking part—four and a half blocks—my eyes, as they say, were floating. Less than a block from the train station, I started looking at doors, but goddamn if none led to retail space. Finally, a woman in front of me stopped at a door and lifted a laminated badge from a lanyard around her neck.

"Excuse me!" I yelled.

Most days I just looked like a pregnant lady, but on that day, I became a *suspicious* pregnant lady.

"I really need to pee," I said, smiling and sweating. "I work up the block, and I'm not going to make it. Can I use the bathroom in your building?"

"Um," she said. "You can ask the security guard."

I followed her into a bare, echoey corridor, at the end of which a security guard sat behind a geometric desk. The woman disappeared into an elevator.

"Hi," I said to the guard, still smiling and sweating. "I just need to pee. Can I please use your bathroom?" I tried to look desperate yet trustworthy.

Possibilities flashed across his face. Would I pee on his floor if he didn't let me use his bathroom? (I might.) Would I sweet-talk my way into the building, whip out the gun hidden in my pregnancy prosthesis, and rob people? Would he lose his job?

"I just need to pee," I said again. "I'm so sorry." I remember thinking, *Why do I keep saying I "just" need to pee? Am I assuring him I don't need to poop or change my tampon?* I stopped myself from blurting out that it was impossible for me to have my period.

Finally, the guard grunted, unlocked the bathroom behind the security desk, and let me in. I never skipped the Panera stop again.

Around the same time, SJ and I went to see *Hamilton*, the egalitarian musical phenomenon only rich people can see because tickets are around $400. I had never heard the music, but SJ was a fan, so there we were one Saturday afternoon, at the Orpheum Theater in downtown San Francisco.

This was when I learned that fetuses respond to the sound of thunderous applause by spasming. Instead of clapping along with the crowd every three minutes OH GOD REALLY AGAIN, I spent the first half of the show rubbing my belly and whispering calming things to the baby, racked with guilt (that starts early) about his developing senses being assaulted.

But what I really remember about *Hamilton* is the line for the bathroom at intermission.

It takes a long time to get anywhere during intermission at any show, but when you're Very Pregnant, you're not exactly slipping through the crowd. By the time I got to the bathroom, the line was LONG.

But do you know what it was filled with? The entire line of people waiting for the women's bathroom? Women and female-identifying people. Women and female-identifying people who knew people who'd been pregnant or had been pregnant themselves.

These people looked at me and were like, Oh, this bitch needs to *pee*.

One woman turned around in line and looked at me. Just looked at me. And this was the kind of middle-aged woman I have known for years, who really wants to get along but finds again and again that she just can't be silent because she sees something that isn't right, or that she doesn't understand, and she has to understand or make it right, and she wants to do things the tactful way but she doesn't have time to think through what that means and she's never done it before anyway so why start now, and she just blurts out what she's thinking or takes the action she knows is right.

I have known for YEARS this is the kind of middle-aged woman I will turn into. We are awkward, we have frizzy hair and "interesting" jewelry, and as long as you can put up with behavior that constantly makes you go WHY, you will find a serious ally.

She came out of line and took my arm.

"You should go to the front," she said.

THANK YOU JESUS WITH THE FRIZZY HAIR.

She walked me all the way to the front of the line so I wouldn't have to do it myself, and I will say that although I was deeply embarrassed—I mean, I like attention, but not for being Preponderously Pregnant and needing to pee—NO ONE made a snide remark or rolled their eyes. It tells you something about humanity that I expected at least one person to protest me cutting the line HELLO GWM FROM CHAPTER 3, and it tells you something else that no one did, and that is: Don't mess with middle-aged women at the intermission of *Hamilton*.

Also, one time at work when I was pregnant, I sneezed and peed through my dress.

Note: One thing pregnant people need to get comfortable with is bodily fluids, because very little about your bodily fluids remains private once you become pregnant. You pee in public (see above), you barf during labor and poop during birth, and this new thing called amniotic fluid goes everywhere during both. After the baby comes, you get really comfortable with baby "spit-up" and mucus.

At some point, all propriety goes out the window. One day when my son was two, out of nowhere my stepdaughter shrieked, "JENNY. I JUST SAW YOU PICK SOMETHING OFF YOUR ARM AND EAT IT."

It starts with pee!

"On a flight when our baby was six months old, my wife was nursing her to relieve the pressure in her ears. My wife was in the aisle, I was in the middle, and a thirtysomething man was on my right. As soon as my wife stopped and turned baby toward me, baby projectile-vomited. It erupted in a glorious arc with surprising reach. With catlike reflexes I shall never be able to repeat, I caught the bulk of the vomit in my hands, but some escaped my clutches and ended up in the lap of the unfortunate stranger who is now probably childless and clean. We called to the flight attendant, who handed us one paper towel—ONE—and went back to her seat. We gave it to the man." —**CHRISSY**, *mom of one*

"When you're a single mom, there isn't a partner to talk to, confer with, or drive you when you've caught a buzz. One night, after my two-year-old went to bed, I give myself a few hits of my vape pen. Then my son starts screaming. I pick him up and he projectile-vomits all over me. I call the advice nurse. She asks for my son's name and birthday and to wait for a call from the doctor. Thirty minutes later (and I'm still high AF), she calls back and says, 'The birthday you provided says your kid is 44 years old.' SHIT. I gave them MY BIRTHDAY. My son starts round 2 of projectile-puking. I collapse on the kitchen floor with him in my arms. We're both crying uncontrollably. Then Bootsy the dog rolls through and starts licking barf chunks off me, my son, and the floor. I am ugly crying and laughing. I experienced clarity and wisdom I never felt before. I knew it was going to be OK." —STEPHANIE, mom of one

9) **go time**
You packed, right?

Most baby books and websites will give you a list of what to bring to the hospital that is suspiciously similar to what you might bring to a luxury hotel for an overnight stay. This is misleading.

The reason they do this is simple: The world wants to protect pregnant people from fear. Awwwww!

This would be admirable if the world also wanted to provide free and equitable prenatal and postnatal care to all pregnant people and allow us to be fully informed about and involved in our health care decisions. Instead, the world tells us to bring cozy socks and leaves out some pretty key information, such as that 50 percent of us will shake uncontrollably and a lot of us will barf.

When it comes to the trip to the hospital—if you are one of the 98.8 percent of US birthing people who give birth in hospitals—you should be informed of what you'll need. Here are a couple of handy lists. Given the level of information you're ready for, pick the one that's right for you.

||||||||||||||||||||||||||||||||||||||||||||||||||||||||||||||||||||||||||||||||||||||||||||||||||||||||||||||||||||||||||||||

WHAT MOST PEOPLE TELL A PREGNANT PERSON TO BRING TO THE HOSPITAL

- A yoga mat
- A yoga ball (don't forget the pump!)
- Cozy no-skid socks or slippers to keep your toesies warm on the cold hospital floor
- Hair ties
- Lip balm
- Snacks
- Your birth plan
- Cozy bathrobe for recovery

- Cozy clothes for recovery (Remember, your body will not revert to its pre-baby state the second you give birth! Bring your maternity clothes.)

- Toothbrush and toothpaste

- Hairbrush

- Deodorant

- Shampoo and conditioner

- Favorite pillow from home

- Camera, phone, and charging cables (extra-long if you know you're having a C-section—you might be far away from an outlet!)

- A tablet for movies or your favorite book or magazine— you might get bored waiting for baby!

- Makeup, so you can take an Instagrammable picture of yourself holding your newborn and keep up the lie for the birthing people who will follow

THE JENNY TRUE CHECKLIST FOR WHAT TO BRING TO THE HOSPITAL

- A thick purple athletic mat (which you won't use)

- A yoga ball and its pump (which you won't use)

- A copy of your birth plan (which will go out the fuck-ing window after three hours of contractions every three minutes and uncontrollable shaking in between)

- Cozy socks (whose use will become obsolete the second you become numb below the waist because you've demanded an epidural with the words, "DON'T TRY TO TALK ME OUT OF IT")

- An eye mask (which you won't wear because did you really think you were going to sleep you dumb idiot fuck)

- *Incense (which you won't be able to burn because it's a hospital and which at no point will you ask to smell because why would you it doesn't make the pain go away)*

- *Headphones and a portable speaker for a playlist you won't be able to listen to because suddenly music is excruciating*

- *Clogs, which are good for catching amniotic fluid when you have a contraction as you're walking across the hall from your temporary room to your private room*

- *Bag of almonds because dry, salty, crunchy food is what you want when you're in pain*

- *White sweatpants. Because a lot of blood will come out of your vagina, and, after the birth, there's a good chance some of it will seep past the maxi pads they give you, and white is an excellent choice for this situation. (Don't forget: White. Sweatpants.)*

- *A block of cheese that will remain unrefrigerated for two days and that you will shriekingly insist on taking back home*

I had a lot of trouble predicting what I might want to eat in the hospital and only knew I would have access to a small refrigerator while I was in the labor and delivery room, but not in the recovery room. Before the birth, I tried to gather some foodstuffs I enjoy, foods that bring me comfort. Cheese has always brought me comfort. So among the items on my list, I brought a block of cheese to the hospital. But I did not eat any of it. I was in the hospital for sixteen hours before giving birth, so maybe I ate something, but I don't remember. After the birth, I was in the recovery room for forty-eight hours, which means the block of cheese was in the recovery room with me, unrefrigerated, for forty-eight hours. I can't sum up those hours except to say that when we left the hospital, I repeatedly asked SJ not to forget the cheese. Bless his heart, the cheese made it home.

- ○ A camera phone so you can remember the time you simultaneously exploded barf from one end and amniotic fluid from the other while lying butt-naked on a hospital bed

- ○ A cooler for all the yogurt you're convinced you'll want to eat while waiting to deliver, but that instead the doula you were privileged to hire will realize she needs so she can take your placenta back to her apartment and freeze-dry it and turn it into iron-rich powder pills, so that ended up being a good idea

- ○ Car seat for the baby

- ○ Outfit for the baby

- ○ A pillow for your ass so the door won't hit you on the way out as a hospital administrator smilingly escorts you to the parking lot less than forty-eight hours after you've given birth, entrusting you and your partner, who also has barely slept, with a newborn in a car on a highway

||||||||||||||||||||||||||||||||||||||||||||||||||||||||||||||||||||||||||||||||||||||||||||||||||||||

THE PARTNER'S CHECKLIST FOR WHAT TO BRING TO THE HOSPITAL

- ○ Pajama pants

the jenny true quiz:
ARE YOU READY TO HAVE A KID?

1 Have you already done everything in life you want to do?

O *Yes*   O *No*

2 Do you have $400,000 in savings?

O *Yes*   O *No*

3 Do you have a separate room in your home for everyone who lives in it and every activity you want to do?

O *Yes*   O *No*

4 Do you have a village? If not, can you get one?

O *Yes*   O *No*

5 Are you in excellent physical health?

O *Yes*   O *No*

6 Are you one of those people who calls their dog a "starter kid" or a "fur baby"?

O *Yes*   O *No*

7 If you answered yes to question 6, what gave you the idea that having a pet has anything in common with raising a kid?

8 Is your dog still alive?

    O *Yes*   O *No*

9 Do you always behave admirably in stressful situations?

    O *Yes*   O *No*

10 Which of the following can you do with one hand while holding a ten-pound bag of flour that has arms and legs and arches its back in anger and cries? (Circle all that apply.)

    a. *Wipe your butt.*
    b. *Make oatmeal.*
    c. *Walk.*
    d. *Think.*

11 Do you like other people?

    O *Yes*   O *No*

12 Do you like children?

    O *Yes*   O *No*

13 Can you think of a child you really like?

    O *Yes*   O *No*

14 Can you think of a child you really don't like?

    O *Yes*   O *No*

This was just for fun! No one's really ready to have a kid. Good luck!

WTF
I'M POSTPARTUM

> "Postpartum care in America is fucked,
> and so are parental leave policies."
>
> —LYZ LENZ, *Belabored: A Vindication
> of the Rights of Pregnant Women*

10) **what is this squeeze bottle thing?**
A guide to the goodie bag you get from the hospital.

The closest I got to getting help with the recovery of my private parts after my son's birth was a nurse recognizing that I could barely stand and putting Preparation H on a Tucks pad *for me* and applying it to my hemorrhoid.

I didn't even know what a hemorrhoid was before I gave birth. Here's an explanation: It's a bunch of swollen blood vessels inside and/or outside your butthole. I experienced it as a soft protrusion that didn't hurt or itch (which it can), but there was definitely something new there, and it disappeared and reappeared for a long time, like two years, every time I pooped.

As the nurse was applying anal cream on a medicated pad to my butthole (definitely her best day that week), I asked, over my shoulder, "Do hemorrhoids go away?"

No answer.

Then: Mm-hmm.

What she could have said was THESE WILL BOTHER YOU FOR AT LEAST THE NEXT COUPLE YEARS SO STOCK UP ON ANAL CREAM AND HEMORRHOID PADS.

The thing is, the hospital is supposed to help you if things go wrong, but for everything else, they just give you a bag of "free gifts" (unless you're lucky enough to get a nurse who will apply Preparation H on a Tucks pad to your butthole). By "free gifts" I mean a pile of items your insurance, if you have it, has already covered, so don't go thanking anyone. These items are intended to help "heal" the body your child just elbowed its way out of.

Let's be clear: *No one will tell you how to use these things.* That job doesn't exist. There may be written instructions on some, but let's be real: You just gave birth! No one's reading any instructions.

This is what happens: Forty-eight to seventy-two hours after you've gone through labor, gone through childbirth, become a parent, and not slept for more than a half hour the whole time *if you're lucky*, someone you don't know will hand you a plastic bag with the following items, shake their head in pity, and go back to watching cat videos on their phone.

Now, for your service, I will list the items you are most likely to get in your hospital goodie bag, with an explanation and instructions:

THE JENNY TRUE LIST OF THINGS YOU GET FROM THE HOSPITAL

Vaginal birth

1. **Cold packs:** These crack-them-and-they-get-cold packs are for you to put in your mesh undies (below) and hold against your swollen, broken vulva and perineum. Yes, it seems weird to hold something plastic with sharp edges against your swollen, broken vulva and perineum, but that's as far as we've gotten with this technology.

2. **Mesh undies:** Stretchy, thin, white underpants that are soft against your swollen, broken vulva and perineum (or C-section scar), large enough to shove multiple cold packs into, and—like regular underpants!—disposable if you get blood on them.

3. **Perineal spray:** Numbing aerosol spray. Manna of the gods. You spray your perineal area and then you can't feel it anymore. I don't even know when my perineal area stopped hurting. They gave me two cans of this and I didn't stop spraying until I ran out.

4 **Mega maxi pads, aka diapers for you:** You will bleed from your vagina after both a vaginal birth and a C-section, and tampons are not your friend right now. Use these.

5 **Sitz bath:** I meant to use this thing but only managed to walk away from my baby one time, for fifteen minutes, to try it (sounds implausible, but just you wait!). The plastic thing that looks like a hat fits inside your toilet bowl (seat *up*). You fill it with warm water and sit on it and soak your swollen, broken vulva and perineum. There's a tube and a hose, but I never figured them out so I can't help you there.

6 **Squeeze bottle:** I never learned what this fucking thing was for until after it would have been useful. It's just a squeeze bottle, so it doesn't come with instructions, and again, nurses and doctors see these things all the time but first-time parents NEED A LITTLE HELP CONNECTING THE DOTS HELLO. You're supposed to fill it with warm water and gently irrigate your vulva after you pee instead of wiping paper against your swollen, episiotomied, Frankenstein-stitched vag. (My friend Katina kept hers and uses it to water her plants.)

7 **Stool softeners:** Before I had my baby, I made the mistake of reading one woman's account of how her first shit after childbirth was worse than childbirth itself. That must have been some childbirth (or some shit). That wasn't my experience, but you'll want to take these pills, because the last thing you want after pushing a large, turd-shaped object through your sensitive parts is to push another large, turd-shaped object through your sensitive parts.

8 **Mega ibuprofen:** Take these.

C-section

My friend Allison, who had a C-section, got all of the above, plus the following:

Meds for nerve pain

One-use dry wipes to pat incision dry after a shower

Mild aloe soap to wash incision

"In the hospital I had gabapentin and oxycodone, plus a benzodiazepine when they were sewing me back up because THAT is a fucked-up thing to experience awake and I was freaking out. They also gave me something SUPER strong after the nurse forgot to put the regular meds in my IV after the surgery and I started to get the shakes from the pain. I kept pulling my husband over and whispering, 'I can't believe I'm this high in front of my mother, my baby, and all of these doctors.'"

—**ALLISON,** *mom of one*

Things for the baby

1 **Snot sucker:** Your baby gets boogers like anyone else, and there's no way to get them out without one of these, but pray Jesus you won't need to use it because the snot sucker, in one plastic mold, is a tool that will ensure your newborn, this precious human who weighs less than ten pounds and whom you want nothing more than to protect, will scream and cry, which will make you HATE YOURSELF. They say you can hurt your baby if you use it wrong, one of many reasons they need to come up with AN ALTERNATIVE.

2 **Hat:** We got a standard-issue cap with alternating blue and pink lines. It's the first thing your baby wears, so no matter your thoughts on the random assignment of color to a binary representation of gender, it's hard to hate.

3 **Blankets:** They've been used by other birthing people, but they've had the shit laundered out of them, and they're free, so TAKE THEM ALL.

11) people still have opinions
You're still doing everything wrong.

Oh, you think now that you had a baby, you know something?

Did you know there are 345 ways to hold a newborn, including cradle, shoulder, belly, lap, and football SAY IT WITH ME CRADLE SHOULDER BELLY LAP AND FOOTBALL and you need to know them all, and when to use each one, or your baby will hate you?

Some other important things: SKIN TO SKIN OH MY GOD SKIN TO SKIN. NEVER let your baby's skin touch anything other than your skin, or your partner's skin, or someone else's skin. Skin to skin is VERY IMPORTANT and you must maintain it at all times or your baby will hate you.

You need to get enough sleep, because how can you take care of someone else unless you take care of yourself first? But the baby needs to eat every two hours, so you'll need to be awake every two hours to nurse, since breast is best (although fed is best), unless you don't nurse and you have someone to help with feeding (although breast is best) (although fed is best), and when the baby goes back to sleep, if you haven't fallen asleep while feeding the baby you must sleep when the baby sleeps, except that when the baby goes back to sleep, if you're breastfeeding, you need to pump, so just in case you don't make enough milk when the baby wakes up you'll have some in the freezer. And if you're formula feeding because you really hate your baby, or your body has somehow failed to produce milk because you're a failure, or your baby won't latch because they're imperfect and they hate you, you'll need to do *that* every two hours, unless of course you have a partner who can do it—but even though you need to sleep, don't even think of formula feeding *because* you need to sleep because FUCK

YOU. Anyway, if you're formula feeding, when the baby falls asleep, you'll need to bring the bottle and all the bottle parts to the sink and rinse them out right away, and then it's only an hour and a half until the baby needs to eat again, and why aren't you in bed? Get some sleep!

At the beginning you need to wear your baby WEAR YOUR BABY with their legs folded up inside your OFFICIAL BABY-WEARING SLING WHAT YOU DON'T HAVE ONE HOW ARE YOU GOING TO WEAR YOUR BABY, because to them they're in the "fourth trimester" and still curled in the fetal position in the womb, but the second they're large enough, you need to switch their position so their legs are hanging down, out the leg holes of your carrier YOU HAVE A TRANSITIONAL BABY-WEARING CARRIER DON'T YOU, and if you don't switch their legs but you do post a picture of your partner wearing your baby in a carrier on your blog, a well-meaning stranger will send you an anonymous message with a smiley face, correcting your baby's positioning, and you will thank her with a smiley face and immediately switch how you wear the baby, but inside you will shrivel and die because YOU ALMOST RUINED YOUR BABY.

If you want to increase your milk supply, everyone knows beer is a galactagogue, but that's a myth and also you can't drink alcohol if you're breastfeeding, unless you time it perfectly either so the alcohol hasn't passed into your bloodstream by the time you nurse or it's completely gone through your system by the time you nurse, but moderate amounts of alcohol won't hurt the baby either way, but don't drink.

It's important that you eat well, especially if you're breastfeeding, because everything you eat the baby eats, so choose a nutritious diet filled with omega-3s for brain health (for the baby), whole grains, fruits, and vegetables filled with fiber (for the baby) but completely devoid of anything that will give the baby gas or cause allergies, so you'll want to avoid beans, bran, broccoli, Brussels sprouts, cabbage, cauliflower, oatmeal, apricots, prunes, peaches, pears, plums, all citrus, peppers, onions, cucumbers, legumes, caffeine, garlic, cumin, curry, red pepper, tomatoes, strawberries, cow's milk, yogurt, pudding, ice cream, cheese, soy, wheat, corn, peanuts, and eggs.

Please also make sure you don't hold a cup of hot tea above the baby's head or hold the baby near a pot of boiling water or hold a knife above the baby or hold the baby near a flame, and make sure the baby's airway is open at all times because they can't hold their heads up and they could die while you're looking RIGHT AT THEM and don't leave your baby in a car and don't leave your baby alone with a pet and don't shake your baby and don't fall asleep on a couch with your baby and don't fall asleep in a bed with your baby and don't let them put anything in their mouths and also SIDS.

12) jabba the hutt was just postpartum
It explains so much.

High on the list of "gets a pass" is postpartum people. Postpartum people have simultaneously brought new life into the world with their very bodies, ensuring the survival of the species, and realized that no one else—and I mean NO ONE—sees it that way.

"It takes two"? HORSESHIT. Sure, it takes an egg and a sperm for a pregnancy to occur, but 100 percent of what happens after that is women (and some nonbinary people and transgender men) doing what we do best: gritting our teeth and waiting for some shit to pass.

Something SJ said to me that maybe he shouldn't have: "You might be able to make a human, but I can make a cabinet! And it doesn't take me nearly as long!"

The realization that our choice to sustain the species, rather than being revered, is seen as our duty and thus taken for granted (see: no universal free prenatal care, no universal paid parental leave, some health insurance not covering postpartum appointments if they don't happen within a prescribed window of time, only two scheduled appointments with your ob-gyn after the baby is born, wherein one gathers one's exploded labia and drags them to a doctor's office rather than someone coming to you) leads to a convergence of feelings: In addition to the love, awe, and wonder, we are treated to anxiety, depression, exhaustion, and, my old favorite, rage!

Which brings me to Jabba the Hutt.

This most famous of villains is known even to those who don't identify as *Star Wars* fans (such as myself). And how successful as a villain: a grody blob with bulgy eyes and bad skin who drools out of his huge mouth, eats live bugs, and acts inappropriately. He is moody, petulant, and sometimes violent.

Sound like anyone you know? Sound like someone whose contribution to the world is not being treated with the continuous reverence and supplication it deserves?

|||||||||||||||||||||||||||||||||||||||||||||||||||||||||||||||||||||||||||||||||||||||||||||||||||||||||||||||||||||

THE JENNY TRUE QUIZ:

Jabba the Hutt or postpartum person?

	JABBA THE HUTT	POSTPARTUM PERSON
Has complicated emotional response to Carrie Fisher's slim bod.		
Does not give a shit about appearance.		
Won't let most precious/valuable thing in the world out of sight.		
Prefers not to be argued with.		
Responds swiftly and mercilessly to any challenge to authority.		
Hungry.		
Thirsty.		
Bit grumpy.		
Laughs maniacally.		
Would benefit from a good night's sleep.		

13) **parental leave**
Fantasy vs. reality.

I'm not going to lie: Parental leave was great.

For five months, I did not copyedit a single word, because I was not at my job as a copy editor at a midsize nonprofit. I did not panic at the thought of speaking in meetings because I had no meetings. I wrote no terse emails to coworkers about grammatical mistakes and anything else that was bothering me that day. I made no demands that the organization's production schedule revolve around my workflow.

Instead, I nursed my son in a car in a rainstorm. I nursed him in a canvas chair hanging from the loquat tree in our backyard. I lay with him on the couch for more than two hours as he slept. I was so in sync with him that once, when I stroked his arm as he lay sleeping on my chest, I felt surprise that I couldn't feel my finger on my arm—that I wasn't stroking *my own arm.*

Friends brought chicken adobo, chicken and dumplings, homemade waffles, sushi, beer, salad. They brought soft, handmade blankets, posed holding my baby in my kitchen and the backyard, brought baby books and gift cards and bags and bags of baby clothes.

For the first time in my life, I bought a membership to an art museum. I walked my perfect baby, who nursed IN THE FRONT CARRIER, past paintings and photographs and pottery and carvings, imagining I was filling his untrammeled brain with Good Things.

I felt proud. I felt strong and capable. When I was alone with my baby, I felt like the best version of myself, as if the other best version—riding in the backs of trucks and on motorcycles through foreign countries, exploring ice caves and feeding grizzly bears, diving with sea turtles and hunting in caves for the world's smallest mammal, eating and drinking delicious things and hearing the sounds of different countries waking up—weren't slipping away.

I was *not* my best self with people who could talk. I fought with my partner (still do!). I fought with the insurance and disability companies (had to—they weren't paying out). I kicked a few things. And when I wasn't at the art museum, lowering my lashes demurely at the approving smiles of the other patrons, I lived in my bathrobe. I got used to being covered with sweat and somebody else's mucus. I didn't leave my house for days at a time, and right at the end of my parental leave—actually, the first two weeks I was supposed to be back at work—I got a horrible, virulent flu, EVEN THOUGH I'D HAD THE FLU SHOT, and couldn't breathe through my nose for five days.

Still, I was lucky. Only a fraction of new parents get paid leave and not everyone qualifies for job protection because of a horrifying lack of federal parental-leave policy. If you're lucky enough to get parental leave, this is what it might look like.

THE JENNY TRUE GUIDE TO PARENTAL LEAVE: FANTASY VS. REALITY

fantasy ⟶

I'm going to meet my friend at the park/mall/café/museum and we are going to have a leisurely picnic/take a walk/eat a meal/talk while admiring my baby.

reality

You are going to be so late, because of a diaper blowout, a clothing change, and an emergency feeding, that you won't even remember to call your friend until an hour after you were supposed to meet and you will never see them again.

fantasy ⟶

(Pre-baby): I can change a diaper. What's the big deal?

reality

You don't understand what ten to twelve diaper changes a day means until you're *in it*.

fantasy ⟶

(Pre-baby): How can a baby create so much laundry? I don't believe it.

reality

How does this baby create so much laundry? I don't believe it!

fantasy ⟶

I will take care of the baby, and other people will take care of everything else.

reality

You mean if I want food cooked, dishes cleaned, floors swept, the toilet scrubbed, and the garbage and recycling taken out, I have to ask or do it myself? How the fuck is it not obvious that I can't do everything myself?

fantasy ⟶ **reality**

I will make a phone call just to chat.   Nope.

fantasy ⟶ **reality**

I will carry out a plan.   You don't have any plans.

fantasy ⟶ **reality**

I will return text messages, emails, and phone calls in a timely manner.   You won't return text messages, emails, and phone calls FOR YEARS.

fantasy ⟶ **reality**

Having a baby will increase my compassion for the world and my interest in everyone else's children and lives.   I'M SORRY ABOUT YOUR DIVORCE. LOOK AT MY BABY! ISN'T HE CUTE? ISN'T HE CUTE?

fantasy ⟶ **reality**

I'll get there on time.   You will never be on time again.

14) all the feelings, all the time
A look at post-baby hormones.

When I was pregnant, SJ observed me flitting about the kitchen one morning and quipped, "You're in an interesting couple of moods."

Poor SJ. He didn't know about *postpartum* hormones.

I didn't know, either, because nobody told me. Even after having a menstrual cycle for a hundred and eighty-five years before getting pregnant, charting my menstrual cycle while trying to get pregnant (WHY WASN'T I ALWAYS CHECKING MY CERVICAL FLUID OMG IT'S FASCINATING), and then *being* pregnant, the postpartum period was when it finally clicked for me: I think I'm [insert emotion here]? Nope, hormones. I think I'm Jenny? Nope, hormones.

A massive shift in hormones—plus additional physiological shifts, including, possibly, circulatory, neurologic, and immunologic, not to mention lack of sleep and an adjustment period for major life changes—is standard for postpartum people. Here's one scenario: While you're pregnant, the placenta and your ovaries create estrogen and progesterone. The second the placenta comes out? BOOM PRECIPITOUS DROP IN ESTROGEN AND PROGESTERONE.

But warnings about the swarm of estrogen, progesterone, prolactin, dopamine, and oxytocin get drowned out by photos of newborns and their adorable smushed faces, wrapped in soft blankets.

Just outside the frame is a new parent staring wide-eyed at their progeny, simultaneously laughing about the funniest, dirtiest joke they ever heard; spiraling about bringing Black sons into the world; loving so hard their heart is exploding rainbows; fuming because someone somewhere is sleeping; and feeling bewildered that they're still in the middle of the race when they thought the race was to get to childbirth and wondering when they get to catch up on sleep to start fresh on this part.

(For trans dads who go off testosterone during their pregnancies—and who may have had top surgery—this period is known as What the Fuck. Becoming a dad for the first time while experiencing body dysmorphia and dysphoria is one more way the postpartum period can suck it!)

Everything I felt and thought right after childbirth was so wackadoodle I couldn't deny hormones. While I was still in the hospital, I had delirious laughing jags because SJ suggested our friend use Photoshop to give him "amazing abs" in all the shirtless photos I was taking of him holding our newborn. Funny? Debatable. But I laughed so hard I had to hold my innards.

I was a mess. Three weeks after the birth, I had a panic attack at home—NOT AS MUCH FUN AS HAVING A MASSAGE AT HOME BUT OK—at the thought that I'd nearly killed my son by laying him on a pillow—a soft thing, which, I read during an unfortunate moment, was not supporting his neck and could have led to him suffocating while I was RIGHT THERE.

Postpartum anxiety isn't talked about as much as postpartum depression, but it's common. In addition to enduring a panic attack, which I didn't recognize as a panic attack until months later, I believed said panic attack was some biological thing that was keeping my baby alive. NOT TRUE. I also believed that someone, mostly me, needed to be awake at all times with the baby so he wouldn't die, and I believed that *this* belief was some biological thing that was keeping my baby alive. NOT TRUE.

In addition to all this, I had a likely-hormone-related breastfeeding condition called dysphoric milk ejection reflex (DMER): Twelve times a day, right before my milk let down, I was treated to an intense wave of sadness, nausea or lack of appetite, and AN INABILITY TO TALK OR THINK WHAT, which went away thirty seconds later when my milk came in. It would have been great if I'd heard of DMER so I wouldn't skip right past "This could be hormonal" to "My life is a bag of dog shit."

Here's a note from my diary-slash-blog a month after my son was born: "I've settled on a word for how having a baby makes me feel: peeled. If I'm not lurching from one room to another in underpants I haven't changed in three days and a maternity bra wide open on both sides like some kind of fetish gone wrong, my post-pregnancy belly hanging out like a plastic bag full of pizza dough, I'm staring into a pair of deep gray eyes that are staring back just as intently and feeling my organs rotate because I don't have room for so much love. On the flip side, I imagine all the horrible things that could happen to my baby—things so medieval and graphic I'm by turns awed and repulsed by how creative my brain can be."

For the first nine months of my son's life, I couldn't listen to or read the news. I couldn't read or watch anything that referenced, even glancingly, the trauma or death of children (try avoiding all fiction and nonfiction that references this and suddenly you realize ALL LITERATURE REFERENCES THE TRAUMA OR DEATH OF CHILDREN WHY). I burst into tears at anything that had to do with violence against or kindness toward anyone.

Only after nine months could I even turn on the radio. Finally, I could listen to podcasts, and I didn't need to listen to moody Drake songs all the way to work, sobbing after having dropped my son off at day care.

I wish someone had given me a pamphlet that covered more than postpartum depression. I also wish someone had given me a box of Fla-Vor-Ice popsicles, but one thing at a time.

THE JENNY TRUE QUIZ:
HORMONES OR REAL THING?

❶ This child's rash could be bubonic plague.
Are you postpartum?

    ○ *Yes. (It's hormones. Stop googling, and call your doctor.)*
    ○ *No. (It's a real thing. Call your doctor and the CDC.)*

❷ I need to have sex with my neighbor.
Are you postpartum?

    ○ *Yes. (It's hormones. Slow your roll.)*
    ○ *No. (It's a real thing. Git after it!)*

❸ My living room needs a makeover.
Are you postpartum?

    ○ *Yes. (It's hormones. Put the vacuum cleaner down.)*
    ○ *No. (It's a real thing. May I suggest a new couch cover?)*

❹ Now would be a good time to run for office.
Are you postpartum?

    ○ *Yes. (It's hormones. Stop reading the news.) (Unless you're California Assemblymember Buffy Wicks! Hero!)*
    ○ *No. (It's a real thing. Put that child in a stroller and get cracking!)*

15) postpartum fashion

If ever there were an oxymoron.

I know what I wore to the hospital: white maternity sweatpants. Apparently I also brought another pair of pants, because I remember having to throw the sweatpants into a garbage can in the hospital after I bled through them in the recovery room. Still, I have no idea what I wore on the ride home, although I remember every second of it, hunched over someone who weighed seven pounds and screaming at every car that got too close.

Knowing me, my coming-home outfit was something practical and not attractive, and I don't mean you'll find a picture of me on Instagram looking charmingly disheveled. The only thing I remember liking about my appearance after my son was born were my calves, since I had decided to make calf raises part of my pre-baby fitness routine and the extra forty pounds helped.

Unfortunately, I wasn't taking pictures of my calves then. Mostly, I was taking pictures of my newborn, and occasionally, under duress, someone else would take a picture of me. When I look at pictures of myself from that time, it's really OK that there aren't more of them.

The problem with postpartum fashion is that you go directly from a body the world has grudgingly agreed to clothe to a body the world is hoping will go away. Eighty-seven thousand percent of advice for new parents is how to "get back in shape" (assuming, hilariously, we were "in shape" to begin with) so the world doesn't have to hurt itself diving away from us on the sidewalk.

THE JENNY TRUE POSTPARTUM FASHION FLOWCHART: WHAT SHOULD I WEAR TODAY?

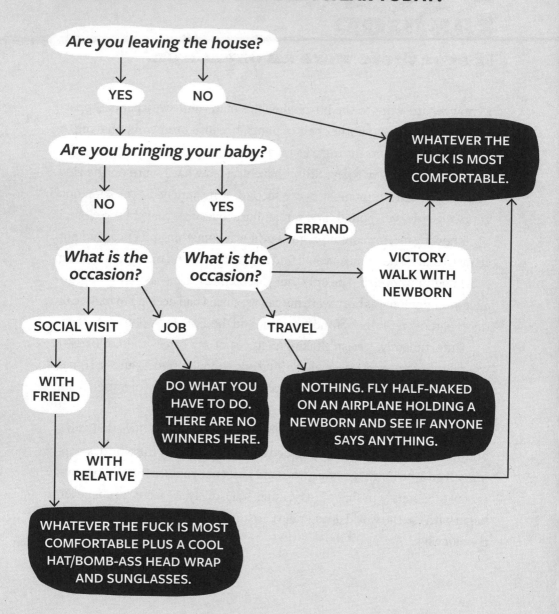

Another phrase we hear a lot in the postpartum phase is "get your body back," which is code for "lose weight." The problem is IT ASSUMES GETTING OUR BODIES BACK IS POSSIBLE.

Here's something a lot of people don't understand: Even the thinnest people who give birth can have abdominal separation, stretch marks, and loose belly skin—all permanent! It's really common! But we are indoctrinated to be ashamed of these changes rather than proud of them, so we cover them up, perpetuating the myth that pregnancy and childbirth are temporary situations, rather than physically life-altering events with permanent physical changes. I can no longer sit cross-legged on a hard surface, because my coccyx is not in the same place it was pre-birth. Also, I have some before-and-after pictures of my boobs if anyone's interested.

"I want to talk about the products, and the procedures, marketed to moms under this notion that we are somehow ruined by pregnancy, birth, and breast-feeding. Also, how said products and procedures can 'fix us.' Fuck that. Fuck them. Fuck the patriarchy. My body created and grew life, then painstakingly pushed it out into the world, and finally produced its sole food source for the first six months. Nothing is ruined. It's fucking glorious."

—**KRISTEN,** *mom of two*

And since no one will tell you: If you nurse, having the baby does not suddenly make your old wardrobe available to you. Any camisole, tank top, T-shirt, short-sleeved shirt, long-sleeved shirt, sweater, sweatshirt, and dress—ESPECIALLY DRESSES, GOD DRESSES ARE THE WORST—that does not offer immediate access to your naked breasts in the form of snaps, a zipper, a V-neck, or buttons (and you're not going to want to button and unbutton twelve times a day, so even buttons are out) are still not available to you. This may seem obvious to people who've been through childbirth, but NEW PARENTS NEED SOMEONE TO CONNECT THE DOTS HELLO.

When I got home from the hospital, mostly I wore the nightshirt they gave me there, because the front had snaps from the neck to the belly. Also I wore leggings, a lot of tank tops, and my bathrobe.

However, SJ insisted on buying a wrap carrier, and this is important. The wrap carrier was seventy-three feet of cloth, and you needed to watch an instructional video to learn how to use it. Once you were wrapped in it with your baby against your chest, you were essentially wearing a shirt (and a baby). Five weeks after my son was born, we took a trip to Sequim, Washington, to visit my mother-in-law and stepfather-in-law. We got up in the dark in San Francisco for the drive to the airport, and the memory of what packing used to be like is enough to tip me into a deep, defensive, narcoleptic sleep: car seat base, car seat, stroller, diapers, wipes, baby shampoo, baby washcloth, a massive duffel bag with toys, books, blankets,

and three pairs of everything, airplane entertainment bag, food bag in case anyone got hungry and thought for a second they were going to buy some overpriced shit from the airplane cart, and purse.

I am sure I laid out my clothes the night before, because I am me, and what I had decided on was clogs, a pair of leggings, a maternity bra, and the wrap carrier. The wrap carrier was warm, I was postpartum (so I was warm), and it was August (so the weather was warm). Also, the wrap carrier was essentially a shirt. NO ONE WOULD KNOW I WASN'T ACTUALLY WEARING A SHIRT.

I recently found a picture of this trip from August 31, 2017, meaning my son was thirty-seven days old. I am sitting in an airplane seat, wrapped in the carrier, with one side down to nurse my son. I am sure I demanded SJ take this picture of me. I am smiling, proud to be traveling with my son for the first time at five weeks, and proud of myself for nursing in public.

IT IS OBVIOUS I AM NOT WEARING A SHIRT. I am naked from my neck to my nipple, including one shoulder and my chest.

You know when you go all day wondering why everyone is smiling at you, and you finally just decide it's because the world is a beautiful place and everyone has finally realized what a great person you are?

Hours later, on the ferry from Seattle to Bainbridge Island, I took myself for a walk to the bathroom, my son still strapped to me. I accepted all the warm smiles on the way, imagining how strong and capable I looked. Outside the windows, Puget Sound glistened in the sun, and these things called trees appeared on every shore (San Francisco has a few bushes draped in plastic bags and a lot of sidewalk feces).

The bathroom on the ferry had a floor-length mirror, so for the first time that day, I looked at myself. Strong. Capable. Then I turned around. That's when I realized I was a half-naked doofus wearing a gray jump rope and a nursing bra.

I peed still wearing my newborn. Then I walked back to SJ and my then-seven-year-old stepdaughter, who were sitting in a booth eating hot dogs.

"I thought I was getting away with something," I said, bewildered, to SJ. "But I'm not getting away with it."

"Oh," he said, chewing. "I thought you meant to do that."

Later that month, I bought a slew of cheap-ass cotton nursing tops, and I wore these, at home and at work, for nineteen months, as I nursed at home and pumped at work.

16) **you want to have sex with this?**
Partners need to chill.

Let me start by saying this: I'm pretty sure SJ and I had sex *more* in the postpartum period than we do now that we have a three-year-old. For some people, such as me, having a young child scrapes all the sexual desire out of you like a farm tool, like a rake or a shovel or a trowel, like it gets in there and scrapes the desire ALL OUT. As someone whose criterion for sex partner once was "what's that like," I'm in the upside-down world: I haven't slept past 7 a.m. in three years, wine has become a bad choice rather than a good choice in the evenings (I now call it "nap in a bottle" rather than "prelude to a night out"), the word *vacation* brings fear rather than joy to my heart, and the pitter-patter of little feet in the hall makes me freeze in place, hoping they'll pass the room I'm in instead of crashing in like the Kool-Aid Man. Also, for the nineteen months I nursed, I had the unique, sex-drive-killing experience of *eating* and *being eaten from* at the same time, and for most of that time, the tops of my breasts were covered in claw marks from my son's fingernails. Sex has been a no-go for a Long. Ass. Time.

I say this because I remember the first time SJ and I had sex after the birth, which was right around the six-week mark, which is when many doctors will tell you sex is "OK." I can confirm: It was "OK." Neither of us remembers much about it, although I do remember that it didn't hurt. I also remember that it felt like relief—like, YAY, this still works!

Now, we have sex six to eight times a year, and I wouldn't say "yay" is what either of us is thinking—more like SWEET, UNDER FORTY-FIVE SECONDS THAT TIME AND GARGANTUBABY'S STILL ASLEEP BACK

TO WATCHING *ALONE* AND FANTASIZING ABOUT HOW WE'D SUR-
VIVE JUST FINE WITHOUT EACH OTHER.

Guess what I learned doing research for this book (what, you think I
didn't do any research?): "There's actually no strong evidence on which to
base advice about when to resume what kind of sexual activity (or bath-
ing, or driving, or lifting, or whatever)," says my friend Karen, a certified
nurse-midwife. "Generally, after an uncomplicated vaginal birth, the rule
is 'whenever you feel like it'—which could be two weeks after birth, or two
years, or never."

But that's *new information*. Historically, the six-week appointment was
when you'd get the go-ahead (or not) for penetrative vaginal sex, if you
were into that kind of thing. Nowadays, the appointment tends to focus
more on birth control options.

Unfortunately, we haven't all been looped in. So a lot of *partners* have
gotten the message that after six weeks, we're open for business.

For the postpartum, female-identifying people in hetero relationships, here's the great thing about men (and male-identifying people):
They don't give a SHIT about the lint in your armpits or the fact that it's
been so long since you showered that your legs stick together. They see
the sweat streaming down your back, baby spit-up souring on your shoulder, a fresh incision across your belly or stitches on your vagina, and Barry
White starts up in their heads. This can be excellent for a new parent's self-
esteem. Still, this means partners can look right past a still-bleeding
vagina. RIGHT PAST.

For people in queer relationships, now is the time when your lived
experience being somewhat different from the heteronormative focus of
all research ever and anything you can read, listen to, or watch will work
to your benefit. (The doctor says I'm cleared for nookie? THEIR RECOM-
MENDATIONS HAVE BEEN IRRELEVANT TO ME IN THE PAST.)

Still: The partner (if there is one) of the person who had the baby needs to understand that THINGS ARE NOT NORMAL WHERE THE BABY CAME OUT, and they may not be for a while.

Here's the thing: Your body is HEALING. And while it does, a lot of blood, mucus, and tissue will come out of your vagina (even if you've had a C-section!), because there's an open wound in your uterus: the place where the placenta attached to the uterine wall. And even though *you* may not need to be told that you're still bleeding and out of sorts, your partner may need to be told that SEX IS NOT HAPPENING. Even if you normally like things in your vagina, the only thing that might be passing through is an IUD so this childbirth shit never happens again.

(Also, for what it's worth, now is not a great time to start dating someone *new*, although the perineal spray might have been a clue.)

Maybe you *want* to have sex, open wound be damned. I've certainly had sex where I knew I was going to hurt the next day. If so, go for it.

If not, here are some examples of the types of conversations you can have to build *intimacy*, so that one day in the future sex may happen again.

||||||||||||||||||||||||||||||||||||||||||||||||||||||||||||||||||||||||||||||||||||||||||||||||||||||||||||||||||||

THE JENNY TRUE GUIDE TO BUILDING INTIMACY WITH YOUR PARTNER, IF YOU HAVE ONE, POSTPARTUM

example no. 1:

After our son was born, SJ and I read him books together, such as *Frog and Toad Together*.

JENNY: "One morning Toad sat in bed. 'I have many things to do,' he said. 'I will write them all down on a list so that I can remember them.'" Ahem.

SJ: Ah. A story and a lecture. How comforting.

example no. 2:

On our first date night without the baby, we immediately fell back into our old rhythms, as evidenced by this exchange from our way home, when SJ was attempting to drive my car out of a parking garage.

> **JENNY:** Why don't you go forward?
> **SJ** (looks down and flips my car out of reverse, but instead of putting us in "D" puts us in some gear called "L")
> **JENNY:** Why are you in L?
> **SJ:** Why did we get married?

example no. 3:

> **SJ** (holding the baby and staring forlornly at the projection screen in our living room, where we were hoping to watch a movie): How do we make it sleep?

example no. 4:

> **SJ:** Have you ever noticed what a dog eating a corn chip sounds like?
> **JENNY:** No.
> **SJ:** Exactly like a person eating a corn chip.
> **JENNY:** Why did you give the dog corn chips?
> **SJ:** I didn't. I gave her toast. But it's dry so it reminded me. One time I was home alone and I heard someone eating corn chips and I was like WHO'S HERE? But it was the dog.

17) is it me or is this the cutest baby ever?
Science says your brain just exploded.

For the first few weeks of my son's life, I didn't know what he looked like. A circuit had shorted in my brain, and I could not compute that the person I held in my arms was my child. I fclt I should recognize him—he was my *son*—but I'd just met him, so I kept taking pictures in hopes that I would recognize him in one of them. Really, who was this human being who had come out of my body? Was this real? SJ and I had sex once, and this person? Impossible.

You can say I was obsessed. I noticed everything—but really, I *felt* everything. My son's smallest change eclipsed my world: His eyes don't cross anymore! He makes a noise when he sleeps! He sucks so hard on the tip of my pinkie it wilts!

These rapid changes increased my sense of disconnect—I was in love but grieving his progress already. I whispered to my newborn that I wanted to clip his roots like a bonsai tree so he would stay small forever.

This phase, this obsession, lasted a long time. I remember showing a coworker a picture of my son, a precious picture from when he was about eleven months old. The picture *moved* me. My son was standing, holding on to a leg of my mother's worktable in the sunroom of their second-story flat in Evanston, Illinois. He was looking up, smiling so his four teeth showed, the sun on his face.

My coworker smiled. He had a young son. But I realized from his polite response that he didn't *feel the picture*. He was thinking about getting back to his desk to do some IT shit. LOOK AGAIN LOOK AT MY BABY. I had been looking at this picture all day, feeling moved by it every time. And this person didn't have the same response.

Here's something you need to know: Other people don't care about your kid, because other people are stupid.

My son is three years old now, and I still feel love course through me when I hold him, and I hold him all the time. Minna Dubin of #MomLists writes about the "unfettered access" to kids' bodies as a highlight of this time. I often wonder how my son will feel about me demanding to hold him naked on my lap when he's forty-five.

At the same time, now that he's three, he is mostly sticky and his farts are for serious. So parental love does conquer all. I'm clear on the fact that I would throw myself in front of a bus to save his life and not feel a thing— no pain, and no fear of anything except him getting hurt instead of me.

I do have goals other than ensuring my son's yellow brick road through life, but ever since my son was born, my cells have changed to make sure I prioritize his health and happiness. It's true: I read it on the internet, and it's called microchimerism. My son lives outside my body now, but he grew inside it, so some of his cells may live on in the parts of me once meant to nourish him: my boobs; my thyroid, wherever and whatever that is; and MY BRAIN HELLO MATERNAL ATTACHMENT I HAD A FEELING HE WAS CONTROLLING ME FROM THE INSIDE HE'S IN THE HOUSE HE'S IN THE HOUSE (I'M THE HOUSE).

This could explain why I love my son through mega-farts, mucus shields, rage bites, projectile vomiting, and forehead bonks that have resulted in one black eye and one bloody nose.

(Apparently I also could have cells from *my* mother in my body, which is much less exciting. Plus, she could have passed cells from me, which were living in *her*, on to my younger brother. Gah!)

I'll put it this way: I know that I love my son, because to me he is the cutest baby who ever lived, and I don't mean that metaphorically. In the same way some people believe in religious deities, I truly believe there has never been a baby as cute as mine.

But here's what I also know: Newborns aren't cute. I mean, yours isn't (mine was!). It's the same with birds and puppies: When they're first born, they're all translucent skin covering huge eyeballs, no hair, and lots of whimpering. Yich. But we think our newborns are cute so we won't leave them on the side of the road once we find out how much work they are. In fact, we'll spend the rest of our lives making sure they have a hat.

THE JENNY TRUE CUTENESS METER

What is cute? (Please arrange in order of cuteness.)

____ A. Mini Lop rabbits

____ B. Koala bears

____ C. Hedgehogs

____ D. Sea otters

____ E. Harp seals

____ F. My baby

____ G. Your baby

ANSWER KEY: F AND EVERYTHING ELSE CAN GO TO HELL.

18) pumping
A love story.

One day, if you breastfeed and you either (a) have a job, and/or (b) want/ need to be away from your baby during a feeding, you will need to become familiar with the "solution" to this: pumping.

Pumping is as fucking medieval as it sounds. You hook your breasts up to a machine, press a button, and are milked. If you're really adventurous or nowhere near an electrical outlet, you can milk yourself with a hand pump.

I put off learning this shit for a long time. I was too overwhelmed with figuring out how to be a parent to learn how to use a fucking machine.

But about four months after my son was born, I watched a YouTube video and learned how to use the electric pump a friend had given me. Before then, I had no idea why she also gave me a box of long, flat plastic bags with measurements on the side, or what the mountain of little plastic pieces and hoses and bottles were for, or why there was a battery pack, or how to use the strapless bra with the zipper up the front and the Velcro in the back and holes where the nipples should be, all of which filled a midsize box.

Here's the awesome thing about pumping: NOTHING. IT SUCKS. Three to four times a day after I went back to work, I would shut myself in the "mothers' room" and milk myself while I cried and watched day-old videos of my baby on my phone. The pump would say different things to me at different times. One time it said, "Let it out, let it out." After a while, I wasn't experiencing DMER, or dysphoric milk ejection reflex, anymore when I *nursed*—but it would show up EVERY TIME I PUMPED. Which meant that, after I rigged myself up, I had to take a deep breath before switching on the machine, because I was literally switching on depression I CAN THINK OF BETTER USES FOR A MACHINE CAN YOU. The wave of sadness and tiredness would be so intense I had to close my eyes. Multiple times I imagined curling up on the carpet. Some of my coworkers brought their laptops into the lactation room to continue working as they pumped. Fuck that. I watched Netflix on my phone.

Then there was the issue with my "output." One of my coworkers was a super producer, and after a pumping session, I would open the mini-fridge BECAUSE THE LACTATING PEOPLE WHO CAME BEFORE ME FOUGHT FOR A PRIVATE ROOM WITH A LOCK A MINI-FRIDGE AND A COMFORTABLE CHAIR THANK YOU FORMERLY LACTATING PEOPLE to store my pathetic two ounces, and I would see *her* plastic bottle filled to the top GOD.

I never understood it: My baby was FAT. His arms looked like five marshmallows pinned together. Everyone commented on it. My baby was *eating*.

But when I went back to work, I could never get enough milk to last him a day, so every week was another episode of the Great Breast Milk Challenge. Each day, when I dropped him off at day care, I had to check to see how much they had left in their freezer ANNOYING FOR EVERYONE. One day, the assistant called to say I hadn't left them enough milk, and I'd said I didn't want them to give my son formula I HAVE NOTHING AGAINST FORMULA I JUST WASN'T THERE YET, I'd said he couldn't eat their baby cereal yet, and he was crying because he was hungry. I sped back to drop off more milk, and then I cried so fucking hard in my car because MY BABY WAS HUNGRY BECAUSE I HADN'T LEFT HIM ENOUGH FOOD. I HAD ONE FUCKING JOB AND I'D FAILED.

You know what would have made it easier? If pumping breast milk were as easy as pumping gas. Let me start by saying that pumping gas is one of my least favorite have-tos, right after showering SO BORING SHAVE THIS WASH THIS WHEN DOES IT END. Pumping gas takes five minutes. You pull up, pay, and this is the worst part: DO NOTHING. These days you can mess around with your phone, but if you don't have one or you left it in your car, you just stand there, read all the text on the gas pump, look at the other customers a little hopefully but not too pointedly, and then stare at the numbers going up on the digital screen, and when they get close to what you want, you put your hand on the pump, and then CLUNK. It's over.

And guess what: It doesn't pinch your nipples! And when you're done, you're really done! Nothing to transfer into a plastic bag, dribbling milk on the top of a mini-fridge and sometimes, horribly, knocking over the bottle or plastic bag and dumping the milk. THERE'S A SCENE IN THE MOVIE *TULLY* WHERE THIS HAPPENS AND I HAVE NEVER FELT A MOVIE MORE.

I pumped in a public restroom a couple of times (that's what the battery pack is for), a completely undignified and anti-parent task and why public buildings should have lactation rooms. Twice in five minutes, the janitor leaned in and yelled, "ANYBODY IN HERE?" Twice I yelled back, "I'M PUMPING. IT WILL BE ABOUT TWENTY MINUTES." The second time he made a noise of disgust. The stall was where he stored his "Caution: Slippery When Wet" sign. I attempted to sit on the toilet, but since I was balancing a pump the size of a cinder block and a hose attachment, eventually I gave up and sat on the floor.

Pumping doesn't save you from letdowns. Multiple times I misjudged when my milk would come down, including once when SJ and I had finally made it out for a date night and were halfway into *Solo: A Star Wars Story*, when I felt my boobs getting full and solid and I tried to pretend it wasn't happening but finally we had to duck our way out of the theater and drive home, me groaning in the passenger seat and SJ groaning in the driver's seat for different reasons.

THE JENNY TRUE LIST OF THINGS I WOULD RATHER DO THAN PUMP

1. Invite all my ex-partners to form a meetup to talk about me.

2. Listen to my dad tell another story about driving a motorcycle across Nigeria in 1964.

3. Have a panic attack.

4. Be on a plane ride with lots of turbulence.

5. Watch someone hock a loogie.

6. Run for the bus.

7. Talk about the latest online multiplayer game with a ten-year-old.

8. Be in charge of keeping someone's plants alive.

9. Drive a car with a manual transmission up a long, steep hill.

10. Ride a bicycle in traffic wearing flip-flops and no helmet.

11. Lick the back seat of a taxi.

12. Clean the oatmeal-encrusted bowls an anonymous coworker keeps leaving in the shared kitchen.

13. Take all the meat out of an aspic and eat just the gelatin.

14. Stay on the phone with an internet service provider for over an hour and get transferred eight times, repeating myself each time to each new person, until I don't have a direct line for the person I'm talking to and then get disconnected without getting my problem solved.

15. Fax.

16. Sit next to someone whose ringtone is "Beep Beep I'm a Sheep."

17. Wear a turtleneck.

18. Put hair gel in my vagina and see what happens.

19. Skin my ankles and knees by shaving too quickly with a brand-new razor.

20. Dice a jalapeño, then take my contacts out without washing my hands.

21. Have a cisgender male ob-gyn.

22. "Sweep" my front steps by blowing the leaves with my mouth.

23. Sit next to someone on a plane who's listening to techno music on earbuds.

24. Wear stilettos.

25. Take the staples out of a thousand manuscripts with my fingernails.

26. Install a dishwasher.

27. Run headfirst into a cactus.

the jenny true worksheet:
A FREE-ASSOCIATION EXERCISE FOR THE POSTPARTUM PARENT WHO DOESN'T HAVE A LOT OF TIME

As a creative writing teacher, I've taught "free-writing," or generative writing, for years. There's no point, per se—kind of like having a kid! Free-writing can be a useful exercise for new parents, who don't often have the time or energy for a creative outlet. It also can help you get your body back and help your baby sleep through the night.

Put aside your internal editor and write your immediate response to the following words and phrases. Then, without looking back, move on to the next one:

1 In Norway, when you have a baby, the government just gives you money.

_____

_____

2 Seven to nine hours of continuous sleep is necessary for healthy brain function.

_____

_____

3 Car seat recall.

_____

_____

4 People who don't have kids telling you how tired they are.

_____

_____

5 Online parent group.

_____

_____

6 Surprise family visit.

_____

_____

7 Choking hazard.

_____

_____

8 Last-minute babysitter cancellation.

_____

_____

9 Hospital bill.

_____

_____

10 Mastitis.

_____

_____

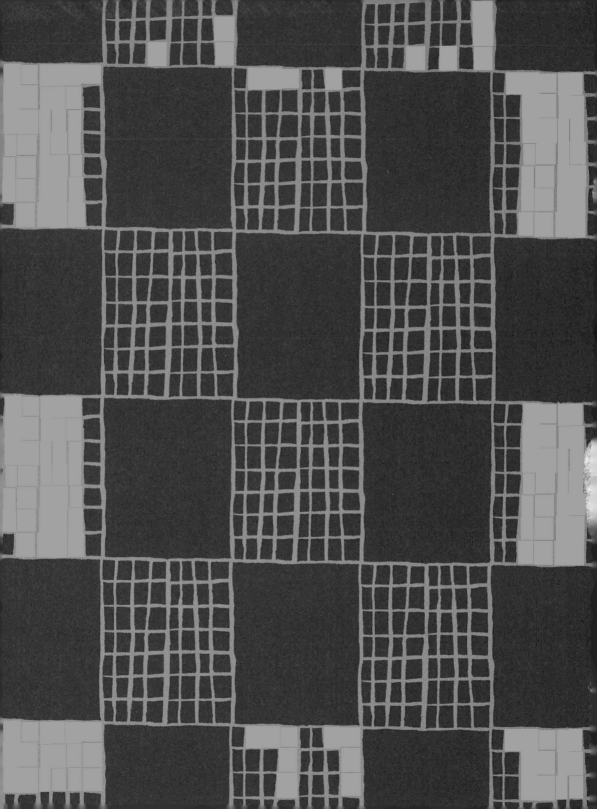

WTF
I'M A PARENT

"Mom guilt is real. When my son got bit by another kid at preschool, I blamed myself cuz I dressed him in an alligator shirt that day."

—STEPHANIE, *mom of one*

19) who am i anymore?
Having a kid puts your identity in the juicer.

I had my son later in life than some—forty. Which means I'd had almost forty years to figure out who I was, after shuttling through some possibilities—gay soft-butch journalist softball player? Straight married coke-snorting graduate student? Divorced anorexic/bulimic marathon-runner world-traveler? I'd finally landed on something that worked for me: career copy editor with a four-door junker, too many books, and some camping equipment, living in a one-bedroom apartment in Oakland, California, with four foster kittens.

It was the happiest time of my life. Sure, I still had 4 a.m. anxiety attacks, generally after too much wine and late-night solo Netflix. But I had friends. I had beautiful neighbors I LOVE YOU FOREVER TOLER HEIGHTS. I bought a bed—a real bed, a KING-SIZE bed—that wasn't a futon or a cast-off mattress from a roommate. I painted my apartment the colors I wanted—ochre and slate gray. It was my level of clean. I had a tub instead of a crappy shower stall with low water pressure. I spent all afternoon making minestrone or ratatouille (two things I haven't made for three years now), listened to podcasts, worked on the novel I'd been writing for ten years, and did ART PROJECTS. FOR FUN.

One night, I brought a twenty-six-year-old home from the club. Let me clear something up: Even though I ended up at a club called Berlin in Chicago after-hours a handful of times when I was in college, I have never been "a clubber" or "someone who clubbed." Like many people, I can't stay awake past 9 p.m. unless I'm high on drugs. But a friend had recently broken up with her boyfriend, so this was our night out.

We danced near the DJ for a short time before I realized my ex-boy-friend—a man who'd kept me up until 4 a.m. listening to Keith Jarrett, who'd studied in Paris and spoke French, who lived in a single moldy room in a converted garage in San Francisco with no bathroom or kitchen but an upright piano, where he played Bach fugues late into the night, who had the kind of sexual hold over me that would have been Bohemian in a prowling-jazz-clubs-late-at-night sort of way in my early twenties but instead had eclipsed a year of my thirties when I was trying to Grow Up and Stop Temping—was ignoring me in a booth.

"Go talk to him," my friend said.

"I'm pretty sure he's still mad I dated his friend."

"He broke up with *you*! And it's been two years."

Persuaded that he *should* talk to me, although pretty sure he *wouldn't*, I made my way through the crowd. I stood at the booth. I tried to say hello. He tried to keep ignoring me. Finally, when it became apparent that I wouldn't leave (because he *should* talk to me, right?), he slammed down his drink, yelled something indecipherable, and shoved his way out of the bar. His friend, my friend, and I followed him outside, where he was attempting to storm off into the night, plaid coattails flapping.

"What the hell?" his friend said.

I stood under a streetlight, thinking it was time for me to start making better choices. Then I went back inside and found a mechanical engineering graduate student from San Diego.

The next morning, when I woke up next to a very handsome young person, I thought: *I'm too old for this*.

It didn't click all at once. I had to go through another relationship and more ambivalence about having kids. Then a good friend whose wife had just had their first kid said, "You're such an adventurer. Kids are the biggest adventure. I just wanted to know what it was like."

OH MY GOD. THAT'S MY MANTRA: "WHAT'S THAT LIKE?"

I was thirty-nine. OKCupid served up SJ within two months. I met his six-year-old daughter three months later and got pregnant three months after that. We got married when I was six months pregnant, and I moved in with him and my new stepdaughter a month later.

Then, in July of 2017, "mother" went from meaning *my* mother— NOTHING TO UNPACK THERE NOPE NOTHING TO TALK ABOUT— to meaning *me*.

A lot of people say they don't remember who they were before they had kids. I remember. I had a lot of free time. I got on planes and went places. I sat in cafés on the weekend. I used an alarm clock to wake up in the morning. I read. I hiked. I had one-night stands because they were fun.

So I remember what I *did*, but becoming a parent definitely did a whammy on who I thought I *was*. It started when I was pregnant. At the time, I told SJ I felt 90 percent like myself, 10 percent not. I couldn't say what that 10 percent felt like. Just not me. I wouldn't call it a pleasant feeling, and the worst thing was that I couldn't resolve it. (Having a hard day being pregnant? Go to sleep, wake up, STILL PREGNANT GOD.)

Maybe I thought the feeling would go away once the seven-pound goiter that wasn't me (Wasn't he? Wasn't he half me?) slid effortlessly and without pain out of my vagina.

Nope. As a friend warned me—at my baby shower, no less—having a kid puts your identity "in the juicer."

Normally, I'm pretty hard-driving. I'm hard on myself and, at times, other people. I thought this nature would transfer to my nature as a parent, that my life would be about rules, sleep-training, and swift—but fair—punishment, that my needs would supersede the needs of my child. OH NO. My son was born, and "who I was" melted away. Now, all I do is imagine how I'm going to sell my organs to finance his rock band and land him the perfect job as a bank teller. I want my child to sit behind bulletproof glass all day, have soft hands, and walk to work from my house, where he still lives.

But this focus on my son had a trade-off: my focus on myself. When my son was two, I drove into San Francisco over the Bay Bridge one day and saw a billboard of someone on a mountain bike—a real adventure-type scene. I don't remember what it was selling, but I do remember thinking, *I can't do that anymore.*

I DON'T EVEN BIKE. I'm afraid of crashing, and I'm definitely not getting on a thin piece of metal with a piece of plastic on my head and going up against some cars.

But what I can't do right now is change my mind about it.

One of the things I wasn't prepared for with having a baby was the screeching halt in my life to anything other than taking care of the baby. I imagined it was gradual somehow. Being pregnant was gradual. Sure, I'd stopped with the whiskey shots and stranger sex and was pretty at peace with it, but I still had solo Netflix and hiking and reading. I still had lazy afternoons reading a magazine and making moussaka. Up until I had my son, I poo-pooed people who said they wouldn't travel until their kids were eighteen. *You just figure it out!* I thought, laughing delightedly at my world-view and looking at plane tickets online.

Then my son was born, and now I know what a nightmare it is just to get a kid to a playground—the snacks, the water, the diapers, the wipes, the changes of clothes, the sunscreen, the hats, the stroller.

After three years, the exhaustion is hard to quantify. It's not the punch in the face of having a newborn. It's being dragged to the bottom of the ocean with anvils tied to each limb, except the bottom of the ocean never comes. Time off is not time off. Mornings and evenings are not breaks. I run errands at lunch. Working from home when my son is at day care is the only thing that approaches relaxing, but I do laundry on my breaks. I order wipes. I meal-plan for the week, then make a grocery list, then pick the grocery store that's the best bet for that list, then organize the list by which products will appear in which order as I walk the most efficient route through the store.

The exhaustion, and the constant running from one thing to the next, makes you do funny things. One morning while I was driving Gargantu-baby to day care, I put a maxi pad on at a stoplight LIKE A BOSS. I DID NOT CARE WHAT A SINGLE PERSON SAW OR THOUGHT ABOUT WHAT THEY SAW.

So my days of taking people home from the club are over (probably).

||||||||||||||||||||||||||||||||||||||||||||||||||||||||||||||||||||||||||||||||||||||||||||||||||||||||||||||||

THE JENNY TRUE WORKSHEET FOR THE NEW PARENT STRUGGLING WITH THEIR IDENTITY

1 Describe your perfect day before you had kids.

_____

_____

_____

_____

2 Describe your perfect day now, but put kids in it.

_____

_____

_____

_____

3 Was that difficult?

○ *Yes*

○ *No*

4 List five things you did before you had a baby that became more challenging after you had a baby.

_____

_____

_____

_____

5 List five things you haven't done in so long you don't even remember what they are.

_____

_____

_____

_____

6 How would you describe yourself before you had kids? Choose three words.

_____

_____

_____

7 How would you describe yourself now? Choose three different words.

_____

_____

_____

20) my child needs an aromatherapy sleep sound machine
Products that prove the world is out to get us.

I'm just going to level with you: If you don't buy the cotton teething rattle for $22, your baby will fall behind the other babies.

If you don't buy the play and activity gym that is literally five pieces of wood propped together with rope and a whole bunch of choking hazards hanging down for $75, then you're not meeting your child's developmental needs.

When you're ready for an aromatherapy sleep sound machine, you'll want to make sure you make the right choice for you and your baby: the essential oil diffuser with Bluetooth speaker ultrasonic cool mist humidifier aromatherapy with auto shutoff, or the white noise sound machine generator aromatherapy natural sleep relaxation therapy for babies with heartbeat, thunder, ocean, rain, summer night, and brook.

Right about now you'll want to decide your politics on amber teething necklaces. Either the world is a warm and friendly place and you are progressive in your thinking about how to soothe your baby's gums and haters gonna hate, or the world is a cold and unfriendly place and you are progressive in your thinking that amber teething necklaces are choking hazards and parents who buy them should be put in jail.

If you don't buy products that say they make your baby smarter, your baby will not get smarter. They will never be able to tell the difference between a French horn and a harp, and they will live in your garage attempting to play the same rhythm on the drums until you die.

By now you're probably familiar with the variety of child carriers and strollers you should buy (or shouldn't buy), but perhaps you are not yet familiar with the variety of pillows: infant support pillows, nursing pillows, baby head shaping pillows, body pillows, multifunction nursing/breastfeeding pillows, and baby loungers. Buy them all.

Babies need special washcloths and later will need special utensils and plates and bowls. They need special fingernail clippers for their nails and special brushes for their hair and special mittens to cover their special hands so they won't scratch their special faces and bibs to catch their special drool and special cloth books and the right sorts of art on the wall to engage their attention with each developmental phase (this changes week to week, so you'll want to have a variety on hand).

If you can't afford or otherwise don't have access to or knowledge about these products, don't worry! There are plenty more to make you feel panicky and less-than.

THE JENNY TRUE GUIDE TO WHAT YOU NEED TO AMUSE A SMALL CHILD

1 Tupperware

2 Wooden spoons

3 An old CD case

4 A paper cup

"The baby industrial complex is very real. We just bought a gift for a friend off a registry that included a diaper cream applicator brush—to put cream on your baby's butt!"

—JASMINE, *mom of two*

21) **who invented this fucking car seat?**
The love/hate relationship that is child safety.

My kid, like all kids, has been trying to kill himself since he was born. At various times he has appeared before me and SJ carrying garden shears or a chef's knife. He got a fat lip from launching himself off a chair at day care. If he's ever standing on something so his head is higher than mine, I need to be ready to catch him, because he will launch himself at me without warning, believing so completely in his safety in the world. He once fought me to let go of him in a swimming pool, under the mistaken impression that he floats.

At the age of one, he gagged on the single piece of food I had ever let him eat in his car seat, prompting a near pull-over on a highway (when I was in my thirties and doing child care for a living, I had to give a four-year-old the Heimlich maneuver—SUCCESSFULLY THANK YOU—and I've never recovered). He stills swallows so many plum and cherry pits I've started to believe this is the reason he resembles both a plum and a cherry.

One morning he disappeared for THIRTY SECONDS I SWEAR TO GOD, and when the house had been silent for too long, I began hunting through rooms and finally found him with my pill cutter open and the razor exposed, thoughtfully trying to get into my Lexapro so he could cut a pill in half for me THANKS HONEY.

Whenever he gets distracted from trying to escape to that playground in the sky, SJ is there to keep the momentum going. Right about the time our son learned to roll over, I started calling SJ "Somebody," and he called me "Somebody Else." For example:

JENNY: Somebody left a baby on the couch and he rolled off.
SJ: Somebody Else was standing a few feet away and could have caught him.

SJ and I have what I would call very primitive, animal-kingdom attitudes toward child safety: I live and breathe the safety of my child, and I'm pretty sure SJ would eat our son if I left them alone for too long. He will take the kids out for long days at the park, a godsend for a writer (me), but he frequently returns them bleeding, bruised, and dragging broken toys.

When our son was just born, SJ and I loved the same lactation consultant at our hospital and always tried to get her on our side during debates. Once, when she was trying to please us both, she started a sentence with, "Children are very...," and SJ and I leapt in at the same time with the word she was obviously looking for:

> JENNY: Fragile.
>
> SJ: Durable.

NOT EXACTLY THE SAME THING AND KIND OF THE OPPOSITE IF YOU THINK ABOUT IT.

Kids are not trying to stick around. They empty medicine cabinets and search under the kitchen sink for mousetraps. They climb on things that aren't attached to walls, and they are ridiculous about stairs. My son pulled at wires, opened kitchen drawers and cabinets, and pulled himself up on the mini-bookshelf.

So when you have a kid, get ready to spend more money and watch more instructional videos just to keep them alive.

THE JENNY TRUE GUIDE
TO CHILD SAFETY

Car seats

Let's start with one fact: According to the National Highway Traffic Safety Administration, 59 percent of car seats are used incorrectly. So even if you get the most expensive one on the market, it can fail in a crash if you don't install it right. Also, car seats have expiration dates, so even though they're expensive as hell, you will not be able to buy a used one from a retailer—no one will take the liability. If you want to save some money, you need to know someone who has one to give away, and then you need to check the make and model number yourself for the expiration date. ALSO, a newborn car seat is different from a toddler car seat is different from a child car seat, so, yes, you may be able to buy one of those toddler/kid combo ones and keep track of how much your child weighs to figure out when to switch it from rear-facing to front-facing, but either way, be assured that you will be acquiring MORE THAN ONE CAR SEAT. Later there are booster seats, which sometimes are investigated by independent news organizations for catastrophic failures. Car seats are a reason not to have kids.

Child gates

Something they don't tell you: When you have a kid, if you didn't have a drill already, you need a drill. There are child gates for doors, the tops of stairways, and windows, because these are all things your kid can fall through, down, or out. One of our beds, on which our infant son liked to play, backed right up against a window, and I had nightmares of him pounding his little fists through the window and dying in a rain of glass. The window was painted shut (still is!), so instead of buying a window gate, my partner measured the window, ordered a piece of clear Plexiglass, and drilled it over the frame (with a drill).

The things that make it hard to open drawers and cabinets

You will be spending a lot of time figuring out how to make sure no one can open your drawers and cabinets, which will save your kid from reaching the knives and aspirin, and houseguests will be so annoyed they will never visit again (win-win!). You will have no idea how many drawers and cabinets you have in your home until you have a baby, and then, no matter how many, you will have TOO MANY.

Toilet-lid covers

Pools, five-gallon buckets with water in them, and toilets are all death traps for kids. Don't have a pool or a five-gallon bucket with water in it. Then, if you're inclined, you can buy a mechanism to make it harder for anyone to lift up the toilet seat lid. It also means that if someone doesn't put the toilet seat lid down, you can prove they are trying to kill your son AHEM, SJ.

Outlet covers

Real talk: USELESS. These are not child safety mechanisms; they're a developmental toy to develop your kid's fine motor skills, because babies don't have anywhere to be, so they have plenty of time to just sit in one place and try to figure out how to pull these out, which they will.

Doorknob covers

I would trade my CAR for these. Your newborn will become an infant will become a toddler will become a taller toddler, and eventually they will figure out how to open doors. Be assured that if you want privacy, you will not get any unless you have locks or doorknob covers, and the second your toddler figures out how to open a door, there is no keeping them from exploring your home while you're asleep.

Caveat: The fact that they can't get into a room you're in only means they will pound on the door and scream, "Mama! Come play wif me! Stop working! These years don't come back!," which is very effective at getting a door open.

22) I already had issues and now this shit

Motherhood is mental.

"What's neurosis and what's maternal instinct?"

—MEAGHAN O'CONNELL,
And Now We Have Everything: On Motherhood Before I Was Ready

Long before my son came along, my life was ruined. I was not the kind of person who made Good Choices: At twenty-two, I peed in a neighbor's driveway, right under his garage, on Halloween, assuring my friends that he wouldn't mind because "He knows me!" How can I sum up the next twenty years? It got worse.

One recent summer, one of my best friends listened to me talk about my relationship and observed, "You sound like a nightmare to live with." I told SJ what she'd said, adding hopefully, "I must have some pretty good redeeming qualities for people to put up with me." "You do," SJ said. He hugged me, and while he was still hugging me, he said, "But you're not a constant pleasure."

I've had a host of issues my entire life (anyone?), but the one I can't shake is anxiety. There is nothing that does not cause me anxiety, and my response to anxiety is anger. I tried explaining it to my therapist once: I have anxiety when it's called for (stepping off the curb without looking and nearly being hit by a car) and when it's not (the moment my therapist opens the door to let me into the room). Same response: a fight-or-flight rush of adrenaline that spikes up my chest and, when it's really bad, spikes down my arms and makes my fingers ache.

It took me a long time to connect the dots and understand that some things in my younger years led to this anxiety and, later, a variety of destructive behaviors. I was a raw, self-loathing nerve for twenty-five years, and the frustrating thing was that when I could finally name my pain, it didn't help. Some things got better, but some things just morphed: Pretty late in the game I started having panic attacks, yay! So, after a decade of trying meditation, running, yoga, getting outside, deep breathing, and everything else the internet tells you to do when you really have a mental health issue, I went on Lexapro with a side of Klonopin, and now I don't have rage anymore but rather a tingly sensation all over sometimes where I'm like, *This is what anger feels like. Hmm.*

These are the major changes in my life since I started taking 15 milligrams of Lexapro every morning: I go to bed at 8:30 p.m. and sleep right through the 4 a.m. anxiety attack about awkward text message exchanges/pointed comments made in meetings. I sleep in the same bed as piles of clean, unfolded laundry. When I drop a small bag of specialty salt on my kitchen floor, my chest does not seize with rage. When I trip over my own pant leg, I do not scream in frustration. I have not hit my steering wheel in many moons. I have become capable of waiting until "the right moment" to mention to SJ my preference that all surfaces in our home do not accumulate loose screws, drills, or piles of business cards that have been through the washing machine. I don't dissolve into angry tears when I walk into my living room and see the life-size plastic skeleton he bought at Walgreens at the after-Halloween sale in 2018.

But I'm getting ahead of myself. Because before I went on Lexapro, I had a baby.

When I turned thirty-nine and started panicking about childlessness and within six months had gotten myself pregnant and in another five had moved out of the best apartment in the best neighborhood in the world and moved into some guy's house in San Francisco and became a step-mother, I was, as they might say, in need of some support.

Lacking that, I went into hyperdrive.

When I look back at my to-do lists from that time, I cringe to remember the altered state of someone trying to control the uncontrollable. For example, I had moved from an apartment into a house, so I sorted through every item in both to make sure I wasn't taking anything unnecessary into my new life and that anything unnecessary in my new life (read: SJ's furniture, clothing, and endless piles of binder clips, rusty nails, and spare change) could be properly dispatched (my mother-in-law helped me combine our bags of flaked coconut—really). I cleaned and sorted. I researched child development stages and natural products. I collected donations from friends, from a crib we never put together and a bassinet we used all the time to everything my kid would wear until age two. I bought baby-friendly nipple cream, diaper cream, baby shampoo, and laundry detergent. I went to breastfeeding and CPR/choking classes and got a Tdap immunization. I tried on the nursing bras. I tried to figure out why the hell anyone would make a shoe for a child who couldn't walk yet. I laundered baby clothes and folded them—again and again and again.

Then my son was born, and I found a new focus for all my anxiety: death!

Certainly my obsession with death started when I was pregnant. I would think about the moment of meeting my son and cry with happiness. But the rest of the time, I thought, *He could die in childbirth! He could die when he's one! He could die when he's forty! He could die AT ANY TIME.* I would crawl into bed with SJ in the middle of the night and cry about my son dying.

When he was born, I really understood that I'd spent forty years worrying about NOTHING. I could have been sleeping! I had lost so much sleep worrying about my out-of-proportion reactions to perceived slights, throwing myself at various people who were already in relationships, tactless comments and inappropriate behavior, obscene gestures I'd made while driving.

None of it mattered or held a candle to all the ways my baby could die and all of which I had to imagine so I could form a series of contingency plans.

For months after my son was born—MONTHS—I was afraid to go to sleep, because I had no way of knowing whether he would be alive when I woke up. It was horrible. But being awake was no better, because then *I* could accidentally kill my baby. For example, I wondered:

1 If I walk away from my baby for forty-five seconds to throw the laundry from the washer into the dryer, will he suffocate?

2 If I leave my baby in the swing for forty-five seconds to put steroid cream on my weeping eczema, will he suffocate?

3 If I take a bath with my baby when no one else is home, will I have a heart attack and drop him in the water, leading to him suffocating?

On the worst days, anxiety sat at the base of my throat like a lump, and my body felt weak and boneless. My appetite went haywire; I couldn't tell when I was hungry or when I was full. Some days, it would charge through my chest like electricity, spiking like one of those machines that measures crowd excitement at a sporting event.

Other days, I would burst into tears at situations that had nothing to do with me. I felt empathy with *everyone*, including people I hadn't met, which was REALLY INCONVENIENT COULD WE JUST GET BACK TO ME AND MY NEEDS? I would look at my family and my home, my partner and child and stepdaughter, all of whom had appeared in my life within a year, and feel dazed with happiness. I had done nothing to deserve any of it and, in fact, had worked tirelessly to ensure that none of it would happen (apparently I need to be "managed" at "weddings" and other "social gatherings" where "respectful behavior" is "expected").

My life has improved since meeting SJ, having my son, meeting my step-daughter, and going on medication. I'm sure my friends would argue that I wasn't a complete nightmare (although I keep a short list of people whose opinions should not be consulted). I have more purpose, and joy, than ever.

But I remember the hard times and have nothing but empathy for people who struggle.

For new parents who don't have anxiety but would like to, here's a primer:

||||||||||||||||||||||||||||||||||||||||||||||||||||||||||||||||||||||||||||||||||||||||||||||||||||||||||||||||||||

THE JENNY TRUE GUIDE TO THINGS TO START WORRYING ABOUT IF YOU HAVEN'T ALREADY

Toxins in the water	Toxins in the soil	Toxins in the air
Your kid loving drugs as much as you did	Your kid driving an automobile among other automobiles	Access to pornography lacking realistic depictions of pleasure and consent
Lightning	Floods	Locusts

23) people still (still!) have opinions
How are you still fucking this up?

Do you work? Who takes care of your kid? Do you worry about other people spending more time with them than you do? Do you feel guilty?

Do you stay at home? Are you rich? How does your kid get social interaction with other kids their age? Do you feel guilty?

Is your job taking care of other people's kids while your kids are with someone else? Do you feel guilty?

Do you have a babysitter? Do you have a nanny? Does your kid go to day care? Is it a family day care or an institutional day care? How did you find them? Do they let your kid watch TV? How much do you pay them? Are you drowning in payments but especially during five-week months so you have to reuse diapers your kid hasn't really peed in and serve the same ninety-nine-cent frozen vegetable medley every night?

Do you have a partner? Do they "help"?

I wouldn't put up with a partner who does/doesn't do [fill in the blank]. My partner does/doesn't do [fill in the blank]. My partner is the WORST. My partner is the BEST.

Are you a single parent? How do you do it? Do you feel guilty? Why are you having another kid? Does it make you feel guilty?

Is your kid crawling? Walking? Talking? How many words? Which words? Can they count to ten? Do they know all the colors? Mine does!

Have you read this book? It's a good book. I do everything this book says. You should read this book.

We got this car seat because it's the best. Which car seat do you have? What led you to that decision? My car seat has a cup holder. Does your car seat have a cup holder?

Have you opened a college savings account for your kid? You should open one now. They're only $3,000 to start.

You'll want to get your papers in order. Your will, your power of attorney, who gets your kid if you die.

I only let my kid play with wood toys.

I got my kid one of those mini-SUVs.

I don't let my kid watch screens.

My kid has an iPad, a laptop, a cell phone, an Xbox, and a VR headset.

You're not childproofed yet? Aren't you worried about them swallowing bleach?

I only give my kid 2 percent milk. I only give my kid 1 percent milk. I only give my kid whole milk. My kid is vegan.

My kid sleeps in a crib. My kid sleeps in my bed. My kid sleeps in their own room. My kid sleeps with their grandmother on a mattress in the living room. My kid sleeps on the fire escape under the stars so they can experience nature firsthand.

Where do you get your kid's clothes? What do you mean, "Kids' clothes are a racket"?

VACCINES VACCINES.

24) traveling with children is a fucking nightmare

Putting the *goddammit* in *vacation*.

In 2019, my family achieved that pinnacle of US class privilege: a family vacation in Hawaii!

That shit is expensive. So, at the last minute, when Southwest started flying to Hawaii, I made the decision that would ruin everything: I booked four tickets on a flight from Oakland, California (where we don't live), to Oahu, and then four tickets on a connecting flight from Oahu to Kauai.

LORD GOD IF YOU HAVE CHILDREN AND ANXIETY PLEASE FORGET ABOUT CONNECTING FLIGHTS YOUR LIFE HAS CHANGED AND YOU CAN'T THINK LIKE THIS IT WILL NOT "BE OK."

LIQUID INCIDENT NUMBER 1: Within five minutes of us boarding the first plane, Gargantubaby's pants (and, next to him, my stepdaughter's) were soaking wet, because I had given him a single-serving, landfill-clogging milk container, and after shoving the straw into the container WHICH IS NOT DESIGNED VERY WELL SINCE THIS IS NOT ONLY POSSIBLE BUT PROBABLE, he had dumped it on himself. We hung his pants from the tray table in front of us and—because for once, for some reason, on a fucking daylong trip, I had not packed him a change of clothes (TO BE FAIR NEITHER HAD HIS FATHER)—he sat there in his diaper.

Gargantubaby proceeded to squeeze his bowling ball of a head between the seat backs, grinning and making faces at the passengers behind us. The woman and her teenage daughter pointedly ignored him. *Hmm,* I thought. *Who are these evil cunts?*

Time passed. Art was drawn; movies were watched. Because Gargantubaby was two, there came a time when he needed to run up and down the aisle three hundred times. He decided that the flight attendants needed to experience him running into their space over and over again. The first time he rushed them (still pantsless), one of them joked, "What kind of flight do you think this is?," endearing me to her and her airline forever. A very tall flight attendant mimed taking his own pants off to give to my son, again ensuring that I will never fly another airline, ever.

LIQUID INCIDENT NUMBER 2: Later in the flight, SJ realized his backpack was soaked through. SOMEONE had left the spigot on the water bladder open, and elevation changed, so explode.

What we didn't realize until a few minutes later was that it had leaked all the way to the seats behind us. Which is where Onion Face was sitting with her daughter. As soon as she discovered the water, she began to flip out in a passive-aggressive combination of huffs, lack of eye contact, deliberately weak assurances that, "It's OK, it's fine," and trips to the back to get stacks of paper towels.

So now we were the family who had hung our laundry out to dry on the tray tables and created a marsh. SJ and I apologized profusely. We offered to switch seats. We offered, twice, to buy the woman a drink (She declined! Not my people). I went to the back of the plane to get more paper towels.

In the end, OF decided to stay in her seat with a plastic bag covering the floor in front of her—proving, once again, that if you don't smile at my kid, that shit will come back to you.

LIQUID INCIDENT NUMBER 3: While trying to get Gargantubaby to nap, I ordered a mimosa. HOPE SPRINGS ETERNAL. After it arrived, Gargantubaby, pissed at the attempt to render him unconscious, kicked the tray table and knocked it to the floor. OH HEY AISLE 23 NEEDS HELP AGAIN.

We landed in Oahu, where I thought for sure I had given us enough time to change flights: an hour and forty minutes. Our luggage came out quickly. We had a stroller, a car seat, four suitcases, and three carry-ons. We started walking, as if we had rolled up our home for the winter and were seeking pastureland.

That's when I realized the Oahu airport is the most massive, most overrun airport I've ever been in, and I've been through Shanghai, Tunis, Chicago, London, Istanbul, and Seoul. Oahu's problem is it's one fucking building with one fucking story, and the Southwest gates are LITERALLY the last gates on one end, and the Hawaiian gates are LITERALLY the last gates on the other end. According to one employee, it takes twenty-five minutes to walk from one end of the airport to the other. MAYBE IF YOU HAVE A JET PACK.

As I have implied, I have anxiety. This makes me extremely unpleasant to work with (EVERYONE IS OUT TO GET ME AND I MUST FIGHT

AGAINST ACTS OF AGGRESSION I HAVE CREATED IN MY OWN MIND) as well as extremely reliable (I MUST MEET ALL DEADLINES OR THE WORLD WILL CREAK TO A STOP, THROWING THE GALAXY INTO CHAOS).

Unsurprisingly, up until July of 2019, I had never missed a flight. So as the walk across the airport got longer and longer, I grew more and more anxious.

We stood in line for the check-in kiosks. We stood in line to check our bags. Anxiety was coming around the corner like a brass band.

The line for security was more than a hundred people long. It snaked out of the building and down the sidewalk. Apparently, this was unusual. I ran up the line looking for anyone to help us. I asked a security guard if she could move us up the line.

"I can't move from here," she said.

"You can't help us?" I asked desperately.

"I can't move *from here*," she repeated. "I don't work for the airline."

I ran all the way back to guest services in the next building. I asked the woman behind the desk if someone from the airline could help us get to the front of security.

"They only expedite for international flights," she said. "But you can just get on the next flight."

"WHEN WOULD THAT BE," I panted.

"Forty minutes," she said.

"THAT DOESN'T SOUND SO BAD," I said.

I walked back to my family, who had moved up in line. The woman in front of us showed us videos of dolphins she'd seen on a tour boat. We paired up to walk past a canine unit. And finally, finally, we made it through the metal detectors, which is when I realized our flight wasn't leaving for another two minutes. OH, THE TRICKY FINGERS OF HOPE.

Leaving my family behind, I sprinted all the way to gate A13, which meant I now was the single person in the Oahu airport either looking stressed out or running. I squirted pee into my pants with every step because of childbirth and got to the gate to see our plane still attached to the gangway.

"MY FAMILY'S RIGHT BEHIND ME," I said. "CAN WE PLEASE GET ON THE PLANE, PLEASE."

The attendant didn't even look up.

"No," she said.

I trudged back to my family. We quickly realized that we had run through security so fast we'd left behind our bag of food anxiety (four sandwiches, vegetables, fruit, cheese, cold cuts, crackers, candy). Security had pulled it aside because my tin of dolmas looked like a hand grenade.

We got the bag. SJ stood in line at guest services to get us on the next flight. I took the kids to a store. We ate chow mein and drank sodas, and my son, appropriately, tore the lei Southwest had given him into shreds.

On the flight to Kauai, we sat in the last row, the only row with no windows. I put Gargantubaby against the wall and let him play with the top of my soda bottle. Just before takeoff, I saw he was about to drop it between the wall and the seat, and because this mattered to me for some reason, I reached for it so fast I punched the armrest. Chow mein surged into the base of my throat. My middle finger was so bruised I couldn't pick up a suitcase for the rest of the trip.

Forty-five minutes later, we were in Lihue. We called a taxi to take us to a discount car rental place, another one of my schemes to save us money, which it did, BUT WAIT: When we got there, I saw all the cars were Toyota Echos, and it looked like all of our luggage was not going to fit into the trunk. I begged the taxi driver, who hadn't uttered a single word and was almost invisible behind his beard and sunglasses, to stay until we'd tried to put all the luggage in our car. He gruffly informed me his work was done here.

"I'LL PAY YOU!" I shrieked.

"The luggage will fit," he said.

"The luggage will fit," SJ said.

The taxi driver left. SJ and I rolled down the car windows, and SJ shoved the luggage into the trunk while my stepdaughter and I kept Gargantubaby from running around the parking lot. SJ installed the car seat and I filled out the drop-off forms. It was, as they say, hot as balls. That was when we realized the air-conditioning in the car didn't work. SJ checked a couple of the other cars. No air-conditioning there, either.

We drove north. I had a fight with the car rental place over text message about the fact that they'd overcharged us and the air-conditioning didn't work. They declined to drive a replacement car forty-five minutes north to our condo. We stopped for juice. We stopped for frozen yogurt. We stopped at a grocery store. We drove to the condo and opened all the windows. SJ unloaded the car while I watched the kids run up and down the stairs.

SJ and I were still wearing jeans. SJ was wearing socks with water shoes because he does not give a fuck. We stood outside feeling the breeze and looking out over the parking lot at beautiful green hills.

"There's a rainstorm in the canyon," SJ said, pointing.

We gazed together, breathing.

"There's a racist lamp in there," I said. It was a figure of a young Chinese field worker on her knees.

"Aha. Thanks for the warning."

We had dinner on the patio. SJ had a beer, and I started a bottle of rosé. We all took baths and showers and went to bed at 9:30 p.m. We slept like babies (all of us) with the fans on, and I woke at 6 a.m. to Gargantubaby snuggling in my arms. The sun rose over the ocean.

the jenny true guide
TO PREPARING YOURSELF FOR
TRAVELING WITH KIDS

Questionnaire

Please answer the following questions before moving on to the activity (below).

1 What are you thinking?

2 Do you understand what you're getting yourself into?

    ○ *Yes*

    ○ *No*

3 Have you read a word of this book?

    ○ *Yes*

    ○ *Sort of. It's hard to focus when I spend all day working, nursing, feeding, changing diapers, working, cleaning, cooking, and working, but I'm trying to read for pleasure. I'm really trying.*

Activity

- Slap yourself in the face while giggling maniacally and saying, "I slap you in the face, Mama!"

- Take a shower (in your clothes).

- Open your wallet or purse and dump the contents somewhere it's hard to get to (out a side window, down a laundry chute, out a car window) and focus on the immediate "Did that really just happen" feeling that freezes time and makes you feel like you might throw up.

- Fill all your suitcases, backpacks, and duffel bags with clothes, shoes, books, and toys, zip them up halfway, pick them all up, and run around your neighborhood without a single thing falling out. If something falls out, start again.

- Have someone pee on you. If no one is available, pee on yourself.

- Mimic a long phone call to an airline, a car rental place, a short-term rental website, or a hotel. For example, spend a morning changing your internet provider. Then change it back.

- Strap yourself to a chair. Instruct your family to kick you, slap you, draw on you with marker, pour liquids on you, and fall asleep on you for five hours.

- Run around in a circle shrieking, "OH NO OH NO OH NO OH NO OH NO."

- Dress all in white. Fill a plastic cup with red wine. Drink as much as possible while someone taps it from the bottom.

Don't clean up. Don't take a breath. You're ready to travel with kids!

the jenny true worksheet:
FUN ALTERNATIVES TO THINGS YOU USED TO DO BEFORE KIDS

Instead of _____, do this!

1 **Taking a vacation . . .**

Desperately try to reattach a piece of toast you have cut for your child who has now decided they want you to Put! It! All! Togedder!

2 **Sitting in a café drinking something delicious and writing something brilliant and profound in a small notebook . . .**

Force 2.5 ml of liquid Tylenol into the mouth of a screaming child with a temperature of 104°.

3 **Having sex . . .**

Eat cottage cheese and leftover popcorn for dinner.

4 **Reading a book or a magazine or something fun on your phone . . .**

Finagle breast milk from a bottle in the refrigerator into an eyedropper and squirt it onto the crusted-over eyelid of a squirming baby with a blocked tear duct twice a day for two weeks (it works!).

5 **Talking on the phone to a friend . . .**

Pin your screaming, crying child to the bed and use a snot sucker to remove the boogers that won't come out any other way because your kid's tiny nostrils are too small for your fingernail and your kid won't know how to blow their nose for at least another year.

6 Slowly doing neck rolls to release your tension . . .

Take fifteen pictures of your baby's rash (Is it a rash? Is it eczema? Is that the same thing?) or cradle cap or birthmark (Is it a birthmark? WHAT IS IT?) and email the pictures to the pediatrician with a hilarious, panicked message.

7 Grabbing your coat, getting your hat, and leaving your worries on the doorstep . . .

Put a half gallon of milk, diapers, wipes, and extra clothes into one tote bag, your lunch in another, library books in another, grab your coat, your hat, your child, your child's shoes, socks, coat, and hat, all of which they have taken off while you were packing your tote bags, and drag everything, including your child, out the door.

WTF
OTHER PEOPLE

"Do you switch off the breasts, Jenny? Is that a thing? I mean, the two tanks aren't connected, right?"

—JENNY'S DAD, *eager to be supportive about breastfeeding*

25) an open letter to people who say, "looks like you have your hands full!"
A fantasy based on a friend's experience.

Dear Asshole,

What did you think when you saw me from across the room? When you saw me, eight months pregnant, struggling to cross this café with two bags and a booster seat, my almost two-year-old daughter appearing and disappearing among the man-buns and laptops, and then, terrifyingly, when another asshole opened the door as if they didn't understand TODDLER PLUS UNSUPERVISED ON A SIDEWALK DO NOT MIX, making a break for the street? Did my voice shrieking her name sound like the siren call of motherhood? Did you feel a motherly glow emanating from the sweat staining the armpits of my maternity dress? When you chuckled as I gasped from the combined pressure on my lungs from the fetus sitting on them and the brace that alleviates some of the intense pressure on my lower back but which also squeezes my sides, and the effort of carrying TWO BAGS AND A BOOSTER SEAT—when you chuckled then, did the beautiful struggle of pregnancy and parenthood touch something inside you, something that inspired you to say, "Looks like you have your hands full!," instead of, for example, offering to:

- Carry one of my bags.

- Carry both of my bags.

- Carry the booster seat.

- Carry one of my bags and the booster seat.

- Carry both of my bags and the booster seat.

- Block my daughter from getting killed.

- Wipe my forehead.

- Massage my back.

- Massage my feet.

- Fan me.

- Pour a bucket of ice water over my head.

DO YOU THINK WE'RE HAVING A MOMENT? DO YOU BELIEVE I OWE IT TO YOU TO MAKE YOU FEEL INCLUDED IN MY STRUGGLE AND THAT IN ADDITION TO EVERYTHING ELSE I'M DOING RIGHT NOW I SHOULD TURN MY HEAD AND LAUGH WITH RELIEF THAT YOU HAVE NAMED MY PAIN?

Also, do you think anyone here doesn't know my hands are full? Look how carefully they stare at their screens so they can absolve themselves of offering to help since they can claim they didn't see me, although I'm the biggest, loudest thing in here and I'm literally right in the middle of them. I'm actually touching three of them, but they're pretending not to feel my belly and my bags. That one is pretending not to feel the bottom of the booster seat pressing into her bare shoulder. Let me press harder. Yes, she's leaning so far over her laptop she can't type but still won't turn around. That's commitment.

Here's the thing. I'm a little busy right now. The time and effort it would take for me to turn my head and pretend I don't hate you is beyond my capacity. I've spent eight months losing touch with everything about my body that feels familiar as the child inside me drains me of nutrients. My skin is blotchy. My hair is thick. My nails grow like a corpse in a horror movie. My upper, middle, and lower back scream different notes. My ass hurts. My feet hurt. My vagina smells like a can of garbage. I can't breathe. My hands and feet are swollen. I have a rash on both legs. My temperature is always high. I'm never comfortable. I can't sleep. My daughter doesn't understand why I can't carry her everywhere and wails and cries, which feels like being eviscerated since I want nothing more than to be able to carry her everywhere. She delights and relieves me but also she is a FUCKING TODDLER and in addition to head-butting me, hitting me in the face, and screaming NO at the slightest suggestion that we DO OR NOT DO ANYTHING AT ALL, she makes continuous concurrent and conflicting demands, such as, "Elmo's song! No Elmo's song! ELMO'S SONG! NO ELMO'S SONG!"

Still, you didn't mean to enrage me. No one does. It just happens that people say things and I feel enraged. You are well-meaning, which is the best type of person. Let me explain.

For the last two years my hands *have* been full. They've been full of shit, puke, soaking-wet diapers, the car seat, the stroller, the diaper bag, my kid, and bags (AS YOU CAN SEE I LIKE BAGS) from the pharmacy, the grocery store, the doctor's office, and countless other establishments, including my home, where I keep a pile of bags I can put things into.

Here is a list of things I would rather have in my hands right now than two bags and a booster seat:

- **A good book.**
- **A vibrator.**
- **A tall, cold glass of beer.**
- **Your bloody, still-beating heart.**

Also, my kid. That kid right there, the light of my life, my sweet angel who is now lashed to a parking meter since I've managed to make it outside, put down my bags, put down the booster seat, and unpack a length of rope I keep in the diaper bag.

In a moment, a young person with neck tattoos will arrive with a drink I won't have time to drink and food I won't have time to eat. You will consider walking past my table on your way to an activity that does not involve children and repeating your wisdom.

So, it's my turn:

- People who say, "Looks like you have your hands full," offer nothing to society and, in fact, detract from its moral core.

- It is appropriate to respond to people who say, "Looks like you have your hands full," with "Looks like you don't. I'm walking/wheeling/limping to the end of the block/that bus stop/that parking lot/that shelter. Will you carry this bag of groceries/push this stroller/carry this car seat/carry this umbrella/carry this large stuffed Tweety bird in complete silence and slightly behind me until I have reached my destination and then fade away without saying another word?"

- It is appropriate to respond to people who say, "Looks like you have your hands full," in any way that occurs in the moment.

Get ready.

26) online forums
Never a good idea (with a note on sanctiparents).

The internet is a (sort of) wonderful thing. I can use it to watch Lizzo do an NPR Tiny Desk concert, watch Idris Elba DJ live, read about what the Republicans and Democrats are up to (or not up to), find a partner, look for a used balance bike for my kid, research composting toilets, stalk high school friends, watch *Ramy* and *Shrill* and remember what it was like to be a twentysomething, and generally educate and entertain myself. Mostly I use it to buy wipes, post pictures of my kid on social media, keep a blog about panic attacks and getting in fights with flight attendants, and order stuff I could walk eight blocks to buy in person.

It also can kind of suck. See: onslaught of bad news, traumatic images, internet trolls, bots, hackers, and unscrupulous tech giants who steal your data and facilitate hate speech.

When you're newly pregnant or a new parent, there's a lot that's unknown. Say you have a question. First, you look around your home. Most of the time—unless your home contains a medical doctor, a child development researcher, or a parenting expert HA HA WHAT'S THAT HA HA—nobody there knows. You might call your mom, your grandma, your auntie, a friend, an advice nurse. You might be satisfied with their answer. You might not.

What you're likely to do—instead of drilling down into a research paper or an advice book the size of an almanac WHOA WHAT'S AN ALMANAC JENNY I HAVE NO IDEA IT JUST CAME OUT—is turn on your computer, open an internet browser, and type in your question.

STEP AWAY FROM THE COMPUTER YOU'RE ABOUT TO GO

THROUGH A GAUNTLET OF MISINFORMATION AND ANXIETY FROM WHICH YOU WILL NEVER RECOVER.

I spent a lot of my early pregnancy on online forums. I was living alone in Oakland, California, newly familiar with all the ways my fetus could die. I was literally afraid that sneezing would give me a miscarriage. So I looked things up.

I'd thought I had a leg up on bullshit. I went to journalism school. I used to be a fact-checker. I used colored grease pencils to identify and underline facts on paper WHAT'S PAPER WHOA AGAIN IT JUST CAME OUT and spent hours online with forest rangers to make sure trail directions were accurate for readers of *Sunset* magazine. I once drove a writer for *Dwell* around the bend because I couldn't verify that the headboard on a bed in a black-and-white movie still was satin, as she so casually claimed in a piece that was about something else entirely ("It doesn't matter!" she shrieked. "Yes, it does!" I shrieked back). I KNOW that 90 percent of what people say and write is not verifiable, and I KNOW the difference between fact and opinion. *Bright Lights, Big City* by Jay McInerney was my bible for a time. One of my most oft-repeated phrases is "I don't do hypotheticals," in arguments or regular conversation. I rarely read opinion pieces. I don't watch TV "news," unless it's YouTube videos of a dancing weatherman in Charlotte, North Carolina, or a BBC commentator getting photobombed by his kids on live TV. I care about people's experiences, and I care about facts, but I make my own decisions. HARRUMPH.

All that went out the window when an ob-gyn entered me in the hospital system as "high-risk" simply because of my age (which, I learned, was "geriatric" at forty WTF) but failed to use that term during any of our appointments, leaving me to come across it in her notes.

How could I be simultaneously "high-risk" and in excellent physical health? Why was it important enough to note in my chart but not to mention to me? What the fuck did *high-risk* mean?

So I went online, because I was living on the knife edge of panic, and I'd stopped seeing that obstetrician. Online was where I found out what I apparently was at high risk for:

- **Miscarriage**

- **MISSED miscarriage (a miscarriage with no symptoms—as in, you don't cramp or bleed, but all of a sudden the fetus dies, which you don't feel but find out about later through an ultrasound, so even if you're not cramping or bleeding, you can go ahead and worry)**

- **About four other major chromosomal defects, all of which ensure the baby's death immediately after birth**

- **Neural tube defects, such as spina bifida (no spine) and anencephaly (no brain)**

- **About a dozen other birth defects that aren't as severe but still pose health risks**

- **Premature rupture of the membranes (water breaking before the baby's ready to come out)**

- **Preeclampsia, a condition that's potentially fatal to the mother**

- **Trauma and/or death for everybody during childbirth**

And guess what? There's an online forum for all of these!

Here's why an onslaught of unverified "information" about worst-case scenarios is not good for you: All that "information" goes straight into your worry bucket, and Anxiety comes to live in your shell. And there's NOTHING YOU CAN DO ABOUT ANY OF THESE POSSIBILITIES.

Another problem with online forums is that, once people solve their issues, they stop posting. Rarely do people who don't have to think about some shit anymore stop back by their online forums to share their success. Would you? I wouldn't! Fuck those people!

> *"After my first baby was around six months, my therapist staged a small, impromptu intervention and told me, 'Kristen, get the fuck off Google.' Now, I stay the fuck off Google."*
>
> —**KRISTEN,** *mom of two*

THE JENNY TRUE QUIZ: SHOULD YOU USE AN ONLINE FORUM?

1 Are you pregnant, and you have a weird rash? What should you do about that?

A. *Call your doctor.*
B. *Call your friend who had the same thing.*
C. *Look it up on a reputable website.*
D. *Online forum!*

2 Are you pregnant, and you're worried about genetic defects or anything else that's not under your control? What should you do about that?

A. *Take a hot bath.*
B. *Take a walk.*
C. *Call a friend.*
D. *Online forum!*

Did you answer D to either of the above? YOU'RE NOT PAYING ATTENTION.

THE JENNY TRUE LIST OF THINGS TO DO BESIDES SCROLLING THROUGH ONLINE FORUMS

- Finish writing your novel.

- Hit yourself on the head with a hammer.

- Hit me on the head with a hammer.

- Call all your exes and cry.

- Eat a mushy banana.

sanctiparents: die, die, die

A sanctiparent is a shitty person who has nothing in their life—NOTHING—except a relentless drive to assert that their parenting is superior. SPs take surreptitious pictures of other parents doing BAD THINGS, such as looking at their phones when they "should" be looking at their kids or "letting" their kids have tantrums, and they post them on social media. They take pictures of child-care workers doing Bad Things and post them on local parenting group sites, saying, "Is this your nanny? She didn't look up from her phone for EIGHT SECONDS and your little girl needed help climbing up the slide. Just looking out!" They use the praying hands emoji a lot, because SPs are infused with the power of the Lord and are chasing down other parents and child-care workers because they are doing the Lord's work. Some White sanctiparents have the curious habit of calling 911 on Black and Indigenous parents—or their children—for infractions of the White Sanctiparents' Acceptable Behavior Code, such as playing with a toy gun, selling water bottles without a permit, cheering at a soccer game, or attending a college tour—endangering their lives.

Examples of what an SP says:

- You're formula feeding? Hmm.

- You're still breastfeeding? Hmm.

- You don't make your baby's food? You're OK with them eating all that sugar and salt and rat feces?

- Your three-year-old isn't toilet-trained? Mine was toilet-trained at two days. It's probably because I did something right and you're doing something wrong.

Do not engage an SP. Do not defend your parenting choices. Anything you say (or, more likely, write in an online forum or parenting group) will lead this person to project their worst qualities—incivility, rudeness, lack of compassion—onto *you*, and, maddeningly, they will assert that their comments were meant for your own good, your kid's good, and the *greater* good.

YOU CAN'T WIN. WALK AWAY.

"We had a friend who said that she never felt like she needed a break from her kid and that it was kind of fucked up for us to feel that way. Her kid literally slept for like twelve hours each night and took a two-hour nap every day. We are no longer friends."

—**CHRISSY,** *mom of one*

27) you call them grandparents—I call them mom and dad

Oh, now you want to tell me how to raise my kids?

When my brother and I were in middle school in Quincy, Illinois, we figured it out: Our parents had us to do chores. We had a regular family meeting then, wherein we divvied up the week's duties. We both noticed that my dad always chose the easiest task—vacuuming—while we got stuck cleaning the baseboards and the bathrooms on our hands and knees. My no. 1 job was getting up from the dinner table each night and fetching the gallon jug of Carlo & Rossi from the floor of the pantry for my dad. I can still hear his self-satisfied lowing: "Jenny—get the wine!"

SJ and I Skyped with my parents, now in Evanston, Illinois, to announce that he had successfully impregnated me. Rose and Dave, peering at the screen with their matching crowns of white hair and wire-rimmed glasses, were so surprised they erupted into applause.

JENNY: The cruel joke is that I have ten bottles of wine left over from my birthday party.

MOM: Time for a visit!

DAD: I'm doing the math in my head, and that's about four jugs of Carlo & Rossi.

JENNY: I find it interesting that my parents are calculating how much of my wine they can drink instead of my due date.

Our parents made us go to one dumb church after another—we even had to be ACOLYTES—until I turned fourteen and refused to go. (My mom started out with Catholicism, then fell down the ladder of orthodoxy to Episcopalianism, then fell further to Unitarianism. Later in life, after dabbling in Buddhism, my parents gave up on religion, and now they just take walks.) They made horrible foods, like polenta, moussaka, baklava, liver and onions, tongue, and rabbit (my dad again, slowly making his way through anything unusual from the local grocery store), when all we wanted was Chef Boyardee and Pop-Tarts. They were always late to pick us up from school, although they more or less showed up, and they made us travel around the world with them so we couldn't be with our friends.

HORRIBLE.

My dad had pursuits that were not child rearing (Rotary, Kiwanis, German band wherein he wore a tufted hat and lederhosen and played "The Chicken Dance" on his clarinet and saxophone). My mom was always doing her dumb art, watercolors and acrylics and pottery and pen-and-ink, and once she had a loom and taught art classes to my friends, which was super embarrassing. She even went to graduate school for book and paper arts, where she discovered performance art THE HORROR and traveled the world to do her embarrassing performances.

And NOW, after all this setting of a poor example, these people want to buy my kid presents. STOP IT ALREADY.

Real talk: There's another version of my childhood that's less charming and more full of human error. But I'm hoping my parents will leave me their IKEA couch when they die, so I'm not trying to kill them now with a tell-all (or am I?). Suffice it to say: Mistakes were made.

No matter how you were raised or by whom, becoming a parent brings up some serious shit. For better or worse, the people who raised you help you get clear on what you're *never* going to do when you have kids, and what you're *always* going to do.

Then you become a parent and it all goes to hell.

My mom had two oft-repeated phrases during my childhood (other than calling me "Brunhilde" when I was in a mood): "I am not the maid!" and "Put it in your book, Jenny." The first: self-explanatory to anyone who has ever been female. The second: the standard response to my adolescent complaints, which were plentiful.

GUESS WHAT MOM I HAVE BOOK NOW.

One thing I will never do: call my kid a name.

One thing I have done a few times, despite the fact that my son is a small child: put him in another room because he wouldn't PICK UP HIS GODDAMN TOYS GOD.

Then there's my dad. He has a strange sense of humor. When he really starts laughing, he coughs and squeaks. The hardest I've seen him laugh was at a joke he was telling that had to do with a parrot being trapped under a rug and somebody hammering it on accident, and it was a pun, and I remember thinking, This is kind of funny? But he literally could not talk.

I'm grateful that both my parents laugh a lot, although my mother laughs the hardest when my dad physically hurts himself, which I have mixed feelings about. Either way, before I had a kid my humor was all about SHOCK VALUE and how many times I could reference sex and cocaine, and there was some biting humor in there about other people and a lot of self-deprecating jokes. Then I had a kid, and it turns out my son's laughter is like sex and cocaine, so I'm always trying to make him laugh, and suddenly I'm a FAILURE. I don't know how to be funny anymore, just like my dad. The things that delight me make my son cry. I insert his name in songs—"GB's song!" for "Elmo's song" and "Baaaaaay-beeee-eeeee Gee-Bee!" for "Baby Beluga"—and my son just stares at me, confused, and then screams and begs me to stop.

So I'm turning into not *one* of my parents, but *both*.

To help other new parents sort through the confounding reality that you are trapped in a cycle of intergenerational behavior, I've created the following worksheet:

THE JENNY TRUE WORKSHEET FOR NOT TURNING INTO THE PEOPLE WHO RAISED YOU

1 What is the most messed-up thing they ever did to you?

_____

_____

_____

2 Do you need some more room? Here are some more lines if you need some more room.

_____

_____

_____

3 Are you still writing? Here are some more lines.

_____

_____

_____

4 What will you never, ever, ever do to your own child?

_____

_____

_____

5 What will you always, always, always do with/to/for your own child?

_____

_____

_____

6 Are you clear on the fact that you will make new and fantastic mistakes you haven't thought of yet?

O   _Yes_
O   _No_
O   _Already there, sister._

7 Are you clear on the fact that parenting is mostly failing?

O   _Yes_
O   _No_
O   _What are you talking about? I'm amazing!_

8 What will you do when you find you have done exactly what you swore you would never do?

O   _Alcohol_
O   _Therapy_

||||||||||||||||||||||||||||||||||||||||||||||||||||||||||||||||||||||||||||||||||||||||||||||||||||||||||||||||

"Having not had an idyllic childhood, I felt like 'motherhood' was a dicey proposition at the best of times. Mostly, it's surreal. Even now, I'll zoom out on my life and be like, 'What in the actual fuck, I have a kid?!?!' It's ongoing."

—**CHRISSY**, _mom of one_

28) you call them grandparents— I call them in-laws

A full accounting of the shit you'll eat for free child care.

I have to say outright that I have the best in-laws—and I have a lot of them. These people married and divorced and married again so many times that my son has six grandparents (my stepdaughter has ten since my parents came on the scene), plus so many cousins I've given up asking who's related to whom, and they're all Communists and Black Panthers (or the children or grandchildren of Communists and Black Panthers). My father-in-law got pepper-sprayed in 2019 by the police, marching for climate change, my stepmother-in-law climbed mountains and wrote books and taught philosophy classes wearing a short skirt while smoking a cigar, my stepfather-in-law babysat Barack Obama (not recently), and my mother-in-law ran off to Tehran before the revolution to teach English.

They are hippies to the MAX.

This doesn't come without its problems. I cannot eat an ice-cream cone or soup around these people without everyone asking for a bite EWW, SHARING WET FOOD. And I am constantly regaled with tales of how SJ, their son and stepson, was unsupervised as a child (walking across a city street in his diaper at age one, accidentally eating a pot brownie at a party at age six, climbing on the roofs of three-story Victorians in Portland, Oregon, at age seven, being hit by a car at age twelve, and GETTING HIT AGAIN, BY A BUS, AT AGE SIXTEEN OMG).

These are the people who want to babysit my son.

I may have mentioned that I have anxiety and am obsessed with death. So the dance of requiring that my son learn everything possible from my inspiring in-laws while negating the message that working headlights aren't entirely necessary can be challenging.

For anyone in a similar situation, I have created a chart to help you figure out the level of risk you're comfortable with.

THE JENNY TRUE CHART FOR DECIDING WHETHER FREE CHILD CARE IS WORTH IT

	OK, fine	No, thank you!
Ice cream for lunch and dinner.		
Placing the child on one's lap in the front seat of a car while driving.		
Hours of YouTube videos of old *Muppet Show* episodes.		
Watching the nightly news.		
Taking the child to a gathering of friends where cigarettes or marijuana will almost certainly be smoked.		
Gardening that involves dirt.		
Gardening that involves shears.		
Playing in a room with Grandma or Grandpa's pillbox full of poison.		

29) the tyranny of self-care

A hilarious concept that blames pregnant people and new parents for what society did to us.

I enjoyed hearing many things after my son was born. My favorite was when a coworker commented, "He looks so alert!," implying a great intelligence in my three-week-old. I loved hearing how cute he was, how much hair he had. I even enjoyed the unsolicited assurance that his enormous-at-birth nose would eventually "go down" (thanks, Dad!).

The one comment that upset me, though—and that continues to upset me—was the entreaty to "Take care of yourself."

It exhausted, and still exhausts, me to field recommendations of how to take care of myself, because (1) this phrase technically, literally, grammatically is in the imperative form—someone is telling me to do something (or, more importantly for new parents, something ELSE), and (2) all these recommendations, taken together, comprise ONE MORE FUCKING TO-DO LIST.

Here's what I think: Instead of telling me to take care of myself, TELL ME WHAT YOU'RE GOING TO DO TO TAKE CARE OF ME.

I understand that mental, emotional, and physical health are important. Oh, how I understand it! But here's the problem with "self-care": Generally, accomplishing it involves asking, negotiating, repeating oneself, insisting, arranging for child care, making additional arrangements, guilt, and sometimes fighting. All this for a ten-minute walk around the block to watch the sunlight on some leaves? FUCK IT.

It's no secret that US society does not support pregnant people and new parents and, in fact, works against them. But it also gaslights them with listicles, making them believe that self-care is not only their responsibility but within their power.

Here's how they get you:

- **The United States has no universal paid parental leave.**

- **After insisting on a gamut of doctors' appointments every month before you give birth IF YOU HAVE INSURANCE, once you have the baby the hospital is all PEACE OUT, BITCH.**

- **Diapers aren't subsidized.**

- **Child care is beyond expensive.**

- **Kids require a lot of other stuff that is expensive.**

- **There is no federal requirement that employers provide nursing mothers with a *dedicated* space to pump with a lock on the door, a chair, a sink, and a mini-fridge, meaning new parents all over the country are pumping in supply closets and auditorium sound booths, hoping to God no one walks in.**

In the face of this reality, a Greek chorus of yogis will entreat you to:

- **Meditate!**

- **Exercise!**

- **Get outside!**

- **Get enough sleep!**

- **Eat right!**

- **Take time for yourself!**

Then they gaze at you with beatific smiles, satisfied they have helped, and DISAPPEAR.

Other countries respect pregnant people and new parents. In China, after the baby is born, people "sit the month," meaning the new parent and baby do not leave their home MY DREAM: JUST OPEN THE WINDOWS AND HAND ME A CUP OF HOT TEA AND A MASS-MARKET MAGAZINE attended to by family or a "confinement nanny" WHOSE JOB IT IS TO TAKE CARE OF YOU AND THE BABY as you avoid cold, wind, and germs; eat warm, cooked foods; avoid tech; and rest, sleep, and bond.

In Norway, as long as you've been employed for six of the ten months before the birth and you meet a certain income requirement, you get FORTY-NINE WEEKS OFF YOUR JOB AT FULL PAY. If you don't qualify for this, the government just gives you $9,374. Then you get a monthly tax-free deposit into your bank account until your kid turns eighteen WHAT.

In Finland, over 99 percent of pregnant people go to ten to fifteen prenatal checkups CAUSE THEY'RE FREE. IN THE UNITED STATES, 6.2 PERCENT OF LIVE BIRTHS ARE BORN TO PEOPLE WHO GET LATE OR NO PRENATAL CARE AND 14.8 PERCENT ARE BORN TO PEOPLE WHO GET INADEQUATE CARE.

You know how you're feeling right now? As you're feeding your baby, or waiting for your bank to refund fraudulent charges from someone who stole your identity, or repeating, "I can help the next customer," so many times you're not sure whether you're asleep or awake? That's when a yogi pops up its head and says, "Feeling down? Low on energy? Go to yoga! Here's a coupon! Down from $35 to $34.75! An hour and fifteen minutes to get back in touch with your body and mind. Do it for you!"

HERE'S WHAT THAT WOULD ENTAIL YOU PATTERNED-TIGHTS DIPSHIT:

- Child care
- Transportation
- Equipment
- Money

- Shaving my armpits
- The mental resolve to walk into a room where everyone else has painted toenails, washed hair, and breasts that don't hang to their knees

Even though a yoga class (or a walk to the corner store for a quart of milk and some Flamin' Hot Cheetos) might not currently be within your grasp, you can do for yourself right now with the following worksheet. It's designed to help you feel better, and all you need is a pen. You can even do it at the same time as other activities, such as crying.

||||||||||||||||||||||||||||||||||||||||||||||||||||||||||||||||||||||||||||||||||||||||||||||||||||||||||||||

THE JENNY TRUE SELF-CARE WORKSHEET

Here are the obstacles to my mental, emotional, and physical health:

1._____

2._____

3._____

Here is a list of celebrities who should help me:

1._____

2._____

3._____

Here is a list of family members who can suck it:

1._____

2._____

3._____

I become most enraged when people suggest that I:

1._____

2._____

3._____

Yogi Whack-a-Mole

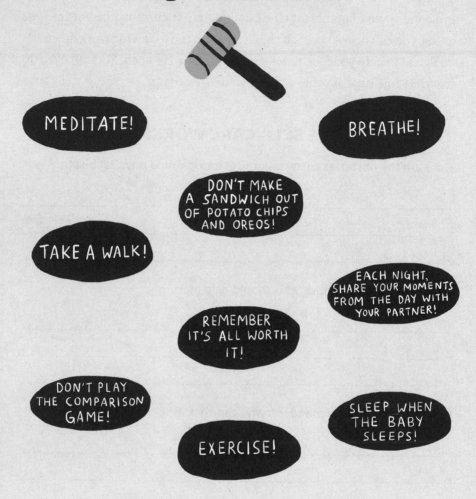

MEDITATE!

BREATHE!

DON'T MAKE A SANDWICH OUT OF POTATO CHIPS AND OREOS!

TAKE A WALK!

EACH NIGHT, SHARE YOUR MOMENTS FROM THE DAY WITH YOUR PARTNER!

REMEMBER IT'S ALL WORTH IT!

DON'T PLAY THE COMPARISON GAME!

EXERCISE!

SLEEP WHEN THE BABY SLEEPS!

"Here's what I think: Make health care and child care human rights for all, and then we can talk about self-care. I mean, I'm totally on board, and put on your own oxygen mask first and all that, but also, self-care is a privilege and I wish we could all experience it."

—CHRISSY, *mom of one*

30) you will be marketed to
Are you even a mom if you don't drink wine?

I am the target market for a whole lot of mom shit. I'm the following things: White, middle class, highly educated, neurotypical, able-bodied. I'm in a heteronormative relationship (regardless of the fact that I once marched topless in the Dyke March in San Francisco holding a handmade sign that read "I LOVE PUSSY" THANK GOD SO MUCH OF MY LIFE HAPPENED BEFORE SOCIAL MEDIA). I listen to NPR and read the *New York Times*. I have subscriptions to *Real Simple* and *Bon Appétit* magazines. One of my jobs is in publishing.

Entire marketing personas are created around my demographic information, and marketers come to where I am (see news outlets, above). Even my Big Issue—anxiety—is part of the profile. I'm not a Karen or a Becky, but those bitches look like me.

Still, when I had a baby, the onslaught of things I was supposed to buy—modeled by the people I was supposed to be—disoriented me.

For example, I don't do beauty. The no. 1 reason I don't wear makeup is I can't fathom putting it on every morning and then TAKING IT OFF every night. BORING. If I *do* ever wear makeup, I leave it on for three days, touching it up a little each morning until I'm finally so sick of it I glob generic-brand cold cream on my face and wipe it off with a wad of toilet paper, reminding myself why I never wear makeup.

So, right there, a major percentage of what's marketed to pregnant people and new parents in the guise of "self-care"—SEE PREVIOUS CHAPTER FOR MY THOUGHTS ON SELF-CARE—is not relevant to me.

We're especially marketed to on Mother's Day (even the marketing plan for this book is based around Mother's Day!). Mother's Day is when we *really* find out who we are and what we need. Before my first Mother's Day, I didn't realize how much I needed scented candles, comfy pajamas, a personalized birthstone necklace, arts and crafts projects, inside gardening kits, decorative plates, and T-shirts, mugs, and "wall art" plastered with photos of my children.

(Still, I had my perfect Mother's Day when my son was two. SJ cut me a flower from the yard and made me an egg and toast for breakfast, and then he kept everyone away from me until dinnertime so I could lie in bed in my bathrobe and watch ten episodes of *Too Hot to Handle*. He bought me a replacement gas cylinder for our SodaStream, and I fucking loved it.)

The indignity doesn't stop at marketing. Film and TV step in to present your options on whom to be (and what to buy), and you will need to become a Mom Trope to be considered for representation.

Before you go any further on your journey as a new parent, you must decide which Mom Trope you're going to be. Here is a handy guide.

THE JENNY TRUE GUIDE: WHICH MOM ARE YOU?

exhausted working mom

CHARACTERISTICS: Eighteen-hour bra, bus pass

BUCKET LIST: Paid vacation

PRODUCT YOU NEED: Coffee maker with individual pods that could fill a landfill in a week

isolated stay-at-home mom

CHARACTERISTICS: Sweatpants, diaper bag

BUCKET LIST: A nap

PRODUCT YOU NEED: Long-distance plan for calling relatives back home and crying about loneliness

wine mom

CHARACTERISTICS: Instagram account for posting snarky mom memes

BUCKET LIST: Girls' weekend in Vegas

PRODUCT YOU NEED: WINE, BITCH

cutely disheveled mom

CHARACTERISTICS: Writing instruments and small toys stuck in hair

BUCKET LIST: Road trip to Sedona

PRODUCT YOU NEED: Throw pillows with vaguely Native American patterns

DON'T SEE YOURSELF?
HERE ARE SOME OTHER PARENTS OF YOUNG CHILDREN THE ADVERTISING, PUBLISHING, FILM, AND TV INDUSTRIES MIGHT WANT TO CONSIDER

(From real people! Thank you to Donnie, Lori, Stephanie, Amanda, Isaac, Kristen, Jasmine, Chrissy, Sasha, Ann, and Jessica.)

trans dad
CHARACTERISTICS: Cuffed everything (shirts, pants, socks)
BUCKET LIST: Baby carrier that works with chest binder
PRODUCT YOU NEED: "World's _____ Dad" merch

single mom
CHARACTERISTICS: Enraged, tired, worn out, stressed, overwhelmed
BUCKET LIST: Child care
PRODUCT YOU NEED: TaskRabbit for all the shit you need to take care of but can't

nonbinary parent
CHARACTERISTICS: Lapel pin that reads, ASK ME ABOUT MY PRONOUNS!
BUCKET LIST: Societal recognition
PRODUCT YOU NEED: Family bathrooms

mom of a child who is not/not obviously the same race
CHARACTERISTICS: Tired of this world and its assumptions
BUCKET LIST: For people to STFU with their assumptions
PRODUCT YOU NEED: T-shirt that says, NOT THE NANNY

queer mom

CHARACTERISTICS: "Tired of explaining queer shit" face

BUCKET LIST: Procreation without sperm

PRODUCT YOU NEED: T-shirts that say, WE'RE BOTH HER MOM

mom of color

CHARACTERISTICS: Constant mental toggling between just relating to regular parenting stuff and representing all POC

BUCKET LIST: Not being the only mom of color at prenatal yoga/babysitting co-op/back-to-school night

PRODUCT YOU NEED: Anything that shows that White women aren't the only ones who birth or mother

adoptive mom

CHARACTERISTICS: Patience for all the people who say you're "good" or "amazing" in a sort of condescending or idolizing way or who say of your kids, "Aren't they lucky!"

BUCKET LIST: For your kids to be able to know they are loved by their birth mom, foster families, and adoptive parents, to feel bathed in love and not rejection or loss

PRODUCT YOU NEED: T-shirt that says, I AM THE REAL MOM

disabled mom

CHARACTERISTICS: Wheelchair, crutches, or nothing obvious because disabilities aren't always visible

BUCKET LIST: Representation in at least one book or movie or TV show or anything ever

PRODUCT YOU NEED: A way to push a stroller in a wheelchair

THE JENNY TRUE WORKSHEET:
WHAT KIND OF PARENT AM I?

Hi! I'm _____ !

Characteristics:

_____

_____

_____

_____

Bucket list:

_____

_____

_____

_____

Product you need:

_____

_____

_____

_____

31) **the myth of the perfect mommy**
Instagram needs to stop.

It's true that social media—from Facebook to Instagram, Snapchat, You-Tube, and even TikTok—has become a place for us to express ourselves, connect, and find comfort in our shared experience.

It's also a place for motherfuckers to lie.

Look at this picture:

This was taken in July of 2019 at the Oahu airport. My family was on our first true vacation, not to visit friends or family—just us. I had planned this trip for months. Look how happy we look (except my son, who is affecting his nineteen-year-old ze-world-ees-sheet look). We're wearing leis. We're smiling (for the most part). Don't we look happy?

If you've read chapter 24, "Traveling with Children Is a Fucking Nightmare," you know I'm panicking in this picture. We had just landed in Hawaii, and since I'd set us up to change airlines, it had begun to occur to me that we might not make our next flight (we didn't). I almost refused to take this picture, but the novelty of SJ asking to take one indicated it might be important. Immediately after he took it, I started running.

The pull of illusion is strong. This is still one of my favorite pictures of our family, even though I know I'm ten minutes from losing my shit. I framed it, and I keep it next to my bed. I also posted it on social media.

The problem with photographs is lack of context. They capture a moment visually and leave everything else out: state of mind, what happened in the moments before and after, the sound of children screaming, the sound of parents swearing and begging security guards to let us go to the front of the line so we won't miss our flight.

The problem with pregnant people and new parents is we like photos for this exact reason. The BIGGER problem is that we use our photos to convince ourselves, and other people, that we are not losing our minds.

This is what I have *not* posted photos of on social media: my panic attacks, the bloody nose my son gave me (I was pretty sure Facebook would take it down anyway), and my naked postpartum body.

This is what I *have* posted photos of: my son and I enjoying a picnic, us running into friends at a local park, before-and-after pictures of a home paint job.

Still, this is what I've posted on my blog: me pumping in a public restroom, my deflated boob, a burst blood vessel in one eye, the black eye my son gave me with a head bonk.

And guess what—PEOPLE LOVED THOSE PHOTOS. I know, because THEY TOLD ME. They liked my shit. They commented on it. They sent me DMs and shared their stories. I have ANALYTICS, too, so I can see spikes in unique visitors.

But I get the most positive responses when I post pictures of myself either smiling or looking foxy (not often) and when I post good news (or when I spin some horrible shit into a lesson learned that ends with a cocktail, such as when my car broke down on the San Francisco Bay Bridge with my son in the back seat and I had to call the highway patrol and was so scared of us getting hit by another car and being pushed off the bridge into the bay or into highway traffic that my hands were shaking).

Still, I'm not an ice cube. I love positive reinforcement. Why do you think I'm writing a book? I want people to like me! But the myth of the perfect mommy hurts, and we do it to ourselves.

You know what I want? I want Instagram to teach us a lesson. I want Instagram to institute a ban on taking pictures in natural light. FLUORESCENT OVERHEAD ONLY. If you've been barfed on in the last twenty-four hours, YOU HAVE TO POST A PICTURE OF IT OR YOU LOSE YOUR ACCOUNT. You can wear makeup, but only if you apply it with your weaker hand.

THE JENNY TRUE GUIDE
TO GREAT LIARS IN HISTORY

michelle obama

in public:
When they go low,
we go high.

in private:
THESE CHILDREN ARE GOING
THROUGH PUBERTY AND YOU
WANT ME TO LIVE WHERE.

eleanor roosevelt

in public:
A woman is like a tea bag—
you never know how strong it is
until it's in hot water.

in private:
DO YOU NEED TO GO PEE-PEE.
DO YOU NEED MOMMY TO
HELP YOU. PULL YOUR PANTS
DOWN SO MOMMY CAN HELP
YOU.

diana ross

in public:
Take a little time out of your busy
day to give encouragement to
someone who's lost their way.

in private:
GET THE FUCK OUT OF
HERE PLEASE I JUST NEED
FIVE MINUTES.

dolores huerta

in public:
We must use our lives to make the
world a better place to live, not just
to acquire things. That is what we
are put on the earth for.

in private:
¿LLEVAS HORAS AFUERA Y SE
TE OLVIDAN LOS HUEVOS? QUÉ
CHINGADOS TE PASA?

winnie madikizela-mandela

in public:
Together, hand in hand, with our
matches and our necklaces, we
shall liberate this country.

in private:
PUT YOUR DISHES IN THE
DISHWASHER NOW OR
NO PAW PATROL.

To help you assess your part in the myth of the perfect mommy, please consider this worksheet.

THE JENNY TRUE WORKSHEET FOR NOT BEING A LYING MOTHERFUCKER

The most real thing I've posted on social media:

_____

_____

The most fake thing I've posted on social media:

_____

_____

I'm a lying motherfucker because:

_____

_____

Pictures of perfect motherhood make me feel:

_____

_____

THE JENNY TRUE PLEDGE TO POST ONLY REAL SHIT ON SOCIAL MEDIA

I, _____, commit to posting only real shit on social media.

   O *Yes. The greater good is important to me.*
   O *Are you crazy? This chapter was funny, but nah.*

32) an open letter to people who say, "it all goes by so fast!"

Dear cruel, coldhearted person,

I know. I know it all goes by so fast. No one needs to be told, "This beautiful moment you're having with your child? This moment before orthodontia, puberty, driving, sex, and drugs? Guess what? Soon it will be gone!"

No one needs to be taken out of their appreciation of the present moment to a pained, future nostalgia when this thing that's happening right now is a photograph. How about this: How about you shut up?

I sleep with my kid every night. It's my favorite time of day, to lie in bed with him as he sleeps. I don't give a shit about the US cultural tradition of having kids sleep in a separate room or whether or not I "should" be sleeping with my partner and his iPhone (God knows he would prefer not to sleep with someone who taps him on the shoulder four times a night to whisper, "YOU'RE SNORING. WILL YOU PLEASE TURN OVER"). I've found something that makes me happy, and, like a drug, I'm going to use it all up.

My son is three. He still reaches for me in the dark (and in the middle of the day) to hold my boobs, the only human on earth who has ever found comfort in these tiny what's-the-points. He motorboats me. He pinches my chin to hold my head steady as he plants a wet one on my lips, telling me, "This is a twue wove kiss," like in *Frozen*. He tells me we're married. He says, "I love to snuggle wif you, Mama. Snuggling is my good idea." I lie next to him, simultaneously feeling wave upon wave of love—like, I *feel the waves*—and anxiety that even though I've finally found him, I can't sleep with him for the rest of my life. How long do I have? I stare at the ceiling and wonder: Until he's five? Thirteen? At some point he's not going to reach for my boobs anymore, or it will officially be weird, and this will all be over, and nothing like it will ever replace it.

So I know it all goes by so fast. Witnessing the amount of progress a tiny human makes in the same amount of time it takes me to find my car is stupefying. I don't need to be reminded.

Thank you.

Shut up.

33) "you look tired"
Stupid shit people say to pregnant people and new parents.

stupid shit people say when you're pregnant

"Are you sure you should be walking/jogging/making choices that have to do with your own body?"

"You're only [fill-in-the-blank] months? Are you sure?"

"You're still at work? Shouldn't you be at home resting?"
(YES. YES, I SHOULD.)

stupid shit managers say to single parents of small children

"People have been expressing how you're always stressed and overwhelmed." —STEPHANIE, *mom of one*

stupid shit people say to parents of twins

"Twins, eh? Double trouble!"

"Two for the price of one!"

"You got it all over with at once!"

"Do twins run in your family?"

"I always wanted twins!"

"Was it natural?" (NO, I GREW THEM IN A VAT.)

"Are they 'real' twins?"

"How do you tell them apart?" (THEY LOOK DIFFERENT AND THEY HAVE DIFFERENT PERSONALITIES. IT'S AMAZING.) —LORI, *mom of two*

stupid shit people say to pregnant, neurodiverse trans dads with clinical depression

An ob-gyn: "With all your issues, this is going to be really hard for you."

—DONNIE, *dad of one*

stupid shit partnered parents say to single parents

"I'm a 'single mom' this weekend—my husband is out of town!"
("I seriously want to punch them in the face." —STEPHANIE, *mom of one*)

stupid shit people say to adoptive parents

A social worker: "Just keep everything fun!"　　　—ANN, *mom of two*

stupid shit people say to parents of boys

"Don't you want to try for a girl?"

"Are you sad you didn't have a girl?"

"Savor them now because men don't stay connected to their moms."

—KRISTEN, *mom of two*

stupid shit people say to queer parents

"Your daughter doesn't have a father? That's so sad."

—CHRISSY, *mom of one*

stupid shit people say when you're a different race/not obviously the same race as your child

"Are you open to nanny in other households?"

"Are they adopted?"

"What does their father look like?"　　　—KRISTEN, *mom of two*

stupid shit people say when you're postpartum

"You don't look like you had a baby!"

- WOULD YOU LIKE TO LOOK AT MY VAGINAL STITCHES AND TELL ME WHETHER IT LOOKS LIKE I HAD A BABY.

- WOULD YOU LIKE TO LOOK AT MY C-SECTION SCAR AND TELL ME WHETHER IT LOOKS LIKE I HAD A BABY.

- WOULD YOU LIKE TO LOOK AT MY HEMORRHOIDS AND TELL ME WHETHER IT LOOKS LIKE I HAD A BABY.

- WOULD YOU LIKE TO LOOK AT MY SEPARATED ABDOMINAL MUSCLES AND TELL ME WHETHER IT LOOKS LIKE I HAD A BABY.

- WOULD YOU LIKE TO LOOK AT MY LOOSE SKIN AND STRETCH MARKS AND TELL ME WHETHER IT LOOKS LIKE I HAD A BABY.

the jenny true quiz:
CELEBRITIES AS ROLE MODELS

When Ali Wong said, "I don't want to lean in. I want to *lie down*," I said:

O   *Me, too! I'm lying down right now!*

When Amy Schumer did a comedy special while having hyperemesis gravidarum (extreme vomiting) and told the audience, "I'm contractually obligated to be out here, guys. I'm not like, 'The show must go on.' I'm like, 'I will be sued by Live Nation. That's why I'm here,'" I said:

O   *Why doesn't Live Nation care about the health and welfare of its pregnant clients?*

O   *MAKE ME LAUGH, BITCH.*

When Meghan Markle, holding back tears, said to a reporter who asked about her physical and mental health after the birth of her first child, "Thank you for asking. Not many people have asked if I'm OK," I:

O   *Sobbed.*

O   *Googled* MEGHAN MARKLE SLEEVELESS SAFARI TRENCH COAT DRESS.

When Gwyneth Paltrow told me to spend $66 on a jade egg to put in my vagina to help with bladder control (to develop a "Kegel-like physical practice"), I said:

O   *Sign me up. I do anything Gwynnie tells me to.*

O   *I'm glad she got sued for that.*

When Gwyneth Paltrow told me to spend $75 on a candle called "This Smells Like My Vagina," I said:

O   *My vagina does not smell like geranium, citrusy bergamot, "cedar absolutes," Damask rose, and "ambrette," but I wish it did, so send me that shit.*

O *I spend a lot of time trying to keep the smell of my vagina to myself, so I don't want it infusing my home, thank you very much.*

When Cardi B told *Us* magazine, "You know when I was pregnant, I used to tell myself like, 'Ah when I give birth, I'm putting a waist trainer right away.' Bitch . . . as soon as I gave birth, I've been so fucking lazy. It's like, fuck that shit. I really can't exercise right now because I can't really move my legs, you know what I'm saying?," I:

O *Stopped trying to "get my body back" and said, "Fuck that shit."*

O *Googled WAIST TRAINER.*

When Cardi B also said, "This postpartum shit is annoying. Like I been emotional all fucking day for no reason. . . . No matter how many books you read or advice I get, ya'll never be read for mommy mode," I said:

O *I'M STILL NOT READY.*

O *If mommy mode includes writing a hit song called "WAP (Wet-Ass Pussy)," give me mommy mode.*

When Cardi B also said, "I still feel like I got a lot of love handles right here. They not much, but I'm used to having a real tight stomach, so this extra skin and shit, it's like, where the fuck you came from? . . . I might get a little lipo, you know what I'm saying? Because you know, I mean, I feel like I could work out and my stomach will go back to what it used to be, but I don't motherfucking feel like it, bitch," I said:

O *"Oh, I need to be at that meeting? I don't motherfucking feel like it, bitch."*

O *"You want me to pass you the salt? I don't motherfucking feel like it, bitch."*

O *" 'Someone' needs to empty the diaper pail? I don't motherfucking feel like it, bitch."*

HOW TO MANAGE A HOUSEHOLD WHILE ALSO RAISING A CHILD

"We blame our personal assistant regularly for all the missed appointments and scheduling snafus—oh wait, we don't have one!"

—ANN, *mom of two*

34) fuck your expectation that I'll manage a household while also raising a child
Did I stutter.

My house looked liked shit after I had a baby. I'd only lived in it for four months, having recently given up the best apartment in the best neighborhood in the world after (unsuccessfully) floating the idea of coparenting from different cities. SJ and I had no nursery or room for Gargantubaby (still don't!), so our living room became a de facto "command center," with piles of laundry on SJ's L-shaped couch, which was already covered in blankets to hide the stains; the piano bench from the piano we no longer owned crowded with pill bottles (iron-rich placenta pills, mega-ibuprofen, Metamucil); and a yoga ball taking up what little floor space remained between his couch and mine.

To be fair, SJ's house looked pretty bad before I moved in. It had stained carpet in the living room and hall; cracked linoleum in the kitchen; dingy paint; a huge, ancient piano so out of tune you couldn't play it; and clutter in every room. He'd owned the house since 2002, moving out after six years and opening it to tenants—who painted the bathroom lavender, one bedroom forest green with brown trim, and another peachy-orange with blue trim—and then moved back in so the tenants became his roommates. The last of them moved out the day I moved in (except our dear cousin, who continued to share my stepdaughter's room).

I'd managed to get rid of most of the literal garbage. And the previous winter, SJ had gone online at IKEA and ordered cabinets and countertops and spent many weekends installing a new kitchen. But when my son was born, the bathroom was still lavender (not OK with me!); our combined couches formed a U against three walls in the living room; and the third bedroom was an unceremonious holding ground for overflow bedroom and office furniture (still is).

I may play all counterculture, but I WANT MY HOUSE TO LOOK LIKE A SPREAD IN *GOOD HOUSEKEEPING*.

I eat up white paint, clean lines, neat trim, interesting wallpaper, and most importantly NO CLUTTER A PLACE FOR EVERYTHING AND EVERYTHING IN ITS PLACE.

Most of what I buy these days is things to put things in: baskets, buckets, tubs, drawer organizers, closet organizers, and counter organizers. After discovering Marie Kondo, I save every small box. Our washcloths go in a box. My legging collection gets rolled up and goes in a box. My partner's collection of business cards that have gone through the washing machine go in a box.

Not every parent is a clean sort of person, or a tidy one, or an organized one. In fact, in some relationships—I've heard—there's a partner. And the *partner* is the clean, tidy, organized one.

But here's the thing: Every mom—shacked up, single, rich, broke as fuck, queer, straight, adoptive—is *expected* to be clean, tidy, and organized.

Three waves of feminism have not stopped this tide. And rather than an equitable division of labor, the world hands us . . . household hacks.

Oh, the odes to baking soda and lemon juice and white vinegar! The paeans to Instant Pots and mirrors that make a room look bigger! The entreaties to wash stuffed animals in pillowcases and store sheets in the room they're used!

NOWHERE IS THERE A HACK EXHORTING THE BENEFITS OF THROWING A SPONGE OUT THE WINDOW AND SCREAMING, "FUCK THE PATRIARCHY!"

I'm not immune to the appeal of household hacks. I want to be told how my life is going to be easier, cleaner, and more organized in seven easy steps. I read certain magazines with a pen, circling ideas and dog-earing pages to tear out later and save in a manila folder. *And I go through them later*, organizing them in order of importance or the likelihood that I will attempt certain hacks in the near future.

The saving of pages and circling with a pen feels like keeping the wolves at bay—and by wolves I mean compulsive thoughts, anxiety dreams, and fear of failure, all of which these magazines created. And since the wolves aren't going anywhere, I'm a sure bet for hacks until I die.

The problem is, hacks will be what kills me. Because at the same time I'm lulled into believing I should just make flash pickles with the vegetables in the bottom of my crisper drawer, thus reducing food waste in my own kitchen and around the world *at the same time*, the time and energy spent trying to do EVERYTHING ALL THE TIME leads to more anxiety and increased inflammation and poor gut flora, which in turn will lead to heart disease, stroke, cancer, diabetes, and Alzheimer's disease, all at the same time.

THE JENNY TRUE GUIDE TO MANAGING
A HOUSEHOLD WHILE ALSO RAISING A CHILD

1 Make a list of household/child-care tasks you've been meaning to do (examples: research the cheapest subscription service for diapers; boil sweet potatoes, peel them, and push them through a sieve with the back of a spoon; clean the mouse droppings out of the cupboards; create/complete car and home emergency kits; make a béchamel sauce; get a compost bin; start an herb garden; vacuum the dryer vent; anything that requires paperwork, a witness, or a notary). Try for ten tasks.

1. _____

2. _____

3. _____

4. _____

5. _____

6. _____

7. _____

8. _____

9. _____

10. _____

2 Look at your list. Doesn't it feel good to have a list of all the things you really should do in one place? Imagine how your life will look once your list is completed. Imagine the sense of satisfaction and relief.

3 Ask yourself these questions:

Why did I make this list?

_____

_____

_____

Why am *I* the one making this list? (These are separate questions; answer them separately.)

_____

_____

_____

4 Fold your list in half. Fold it in half again, and half again, until you have a tight, wadded-up wedge of paper. Hold it by a corner, shaking. Now stomp around your home until you find another adult, or, if there is none, find one in your neighborhood, and when you do, scream, "SHOVE IT UP YOUR ASS."

5 It's Miller time!

35) fuck cooking
You do it.

I named the period directly after my son was born "Mom Eats Last." By the time I would finally sit down to eat, my son would cry to nurse. I began keeping track, and during one harrowing stretch, this happened five meals in a row. I joked that the baby was eating me alive. It wasn't a joke.

I remember one "meal" in particular, in Sequim, Washington, where SJ and I had taken the kids to visit his mother and stepfather on their farm in the shadow of the Olympic Mountains. It was a former gathering place for blacklisted Communist intellectuals where Pete Seeger had played the banjo. Gargantubaby was five weeks old. I took a picture of him on a sofa chair surrounded by the diapers he'd used during the night and noted that, in a former life, I'd wake up and count the empty beer bottles to see what kind of night I'd had. Now it was diapers.

It was the summer of raspberry mead, fresh corn, and peaches. FOR EVERYONE ELSE.

At home in San Francisco, I'd taken to eating and nursing at the same time. *Fuck it*, I'd think: He's hungry, I'm hungry. We were one big mammalian machine. And breastfeeding in public was my *thing*. I'd nursed him everywhere, including in the front row of a church.

But here, in Sequim, under the polite gaze of my new in-laws, I suddenly felt shy—not a normal feeling for me.

"I'm sorry," I said, pushing my chair back from the table and standing with my increasingly agitated newborn. "I'm going to take him to the bedroom to feed him."

"Don't be sorry," SJ said, his mouth full of something delicious. "Do what you have to do."

I looked at SJ meaningfully.

"I'm not going to eat right now because I have to feed our son," I said.

"Don't worry!" SJ washed down his food with a cold beer. "We'll leave some food for you."

That day I learned that the familiar sounds of cutlery clinking in another room can send a person into despair. I remember feeling not only hungry but enraged that anyone else in the world—OK, SJ—was eating when I was the one who needed food since I was keeping the baby alive with my body.

When Gargantubaby was five months old, my dad visited from Evanston, Illinois. He was more supportive.

> **DAVE** (taking the baby so I could eat lunch): Come here, baby. She needs to make some more milk, so she needs some silage.

silage: fodder (such as hay or corn) converted into succulent feed *for livestock* through processes of anaerobic bacterial fermentation (as in a silo)

I visited my parents in Illinois. My mom was less supportive.

> **ROSE:** You need to eat more vegetables.
>
> **JENNY** (tiredly): I'm always holding him. I don't always get a choice of what to eat.

Mom gives me a look.

> **JENNY:** I'm doing the best I can.
>
> **ROSE** (speaking to me through the baby): But babies can be put down. (Pauses, gazing at the baby. Still talking to me and still holding the baby.) I put you down. Maybe you weren't as much fun.

Still, I exclusively breastfed right up until the last day I could, right up until the end of six months, when you're really supposed to start giving babies "real" food, because I was so overwhelmed with not sleeping and starting work and being aware of my son 100 percent of the time that the thought of making a whole new set of decisions paralyzed me. I'd already learned how to use the wrap carrier and the breast pump. How many YouTube videos can one new parent watch?

Breastfeeding—for all the exhaustion and thirst and hunger and sore nipples and dysphoric milk ejection reflex—was straightforward, and free. Generally, my baby let me know when he was ready to eat and when he was done. I didn't have to think about it.

Food would be different. Food was going to require the mental load of planning, then the physical labor of preparing, feeding, and cleaning up. I wasn't excited about feeding my son food. And it showed: At least twice, SJ and I weren't able to put Gargantubaby to sleep, and around 10:30 p.m. we looked at each other, exhausted, and had this conversation:

JENNY: Did we feed him dinner?

SJ: Oh. Not really.

JENNY: Lunch?

SJ: Well. We gave him part of that falafel.

JENNY: Shit.

First, there was the mashed phase. We went the natural route, so mashed shit—bananas, avocadoes, sweet potatoes—took over our kitchen, along with some pureed shit—peas, carrots, prunes—and some liquidy shit that got everywhere: infant cereal, yogurt. Never in my life has "simple" food required more preparation. (They call it "strained" for a reason!) SJ took over this part because I did not care—I'd been the only one feeding him for six months, so I was not about to steam some shit and push it through a sieve. The only good thing about this period was scrambled eggs.

Now, since most of our kid's teeth are in, he eats whatever we eat, with some adaptations (nothing spicy, and his vegetable is frozen peas). Our

routine: Make his plate first from whatever's on the stove, then stick it in the freezer to cool while we serve everyone else.

I have found myself saying things to my son I never would have before, such as, "You can't live on a diet of cheese alone" WHAT YES YOU CAN REMEMBER YOUR THIRTIES. He lives for bread products: He regularly asks for "soft cwackers," whatever the fuck those are, and "wiggly bwead," which we recently figured out means "regular bread," aka not toast. He also often requests—my crowning achievement—"fwozen stuff." His major food groups are crackers and frozen blueberries, and he's fat and happy (unless he's malnourished—I should check on that).

But the constant food preparation and everything that goes with it—planning, listing, shopping—was something else I was not prepared for when I was single and spending forty-five minutes each night preparing the perfect salad for one.

Spoiler alert: SJ is a great cook, although he tries to put hamburger in everything. But he can throw a bunch of stuff in a pan and make it taste pretty good to four people in the age range of three to fifty-two, and he can bake, so unless I decide I really want to make something from a recipe, he is on cooking duty.

For the times SJ is not available and I'm forced to feed people, I use household hacks.

THEIR HACKS

- A STEP-BY-STEP GUIDE TO FREEZING BREAD CORRECTLY (an actual headline)

JENNY TRUE'S HACKS FOR FEEDING A CHILD

- 8 Reasons Variety Is Not the Priority They Say It Is

- 11 Smoothies That Will Break You with the Labor Required

- 3 Things to Do with Peanut Butter That Are Not Eating

- Guilt vs. Sanity: Your Relationship with Packaged Food

- 7 Foods You Can Just Cut the Mold Off

- 344 Choking Hazards You Can Find in Your Own Kitchen

- 27 Foods You Can Melt Cheese Over and Call It a Day

- Top 2 Reasons You Will Always Long for the Infant Cereal Phase
  1) Pour cereal.
  2) Add water.

36) fuck cleaning
You do it.

There are some chores I hate less than others. SJ hates laundry because of all the tasks involved: sorting, washing, drying, folding, putting away. He finds it overwhelming and often doesn't make it past step 1 before the demands of *Sid Meier's Civilization* take over. I don't hate laundry, because you don't get dirty or wet, and you can do it in small steps instead of needing to block off large chunks of time. And then: clean tank tops and flannel shirts from Goodwill!

SJ doesn't mind washing pots and pans, but I hate it. For him, it's one long task he can complete while listening to a podcast. For me, I have eczema on my hands, I don't like putting on gloves to protect my hands, and I don't like getting wet.

Organizing: Now, I can get with that. I can organize, declutter, and sort all day. Organizing refreshes your space, uses critical-thinking skills, gets the blood pumping. I love nothing better than picking up a thing and putting it somewhere else, somewhere better, somewhere it *should* be.

But overall, cleaning SUCKS. Still, we do it (SOME OF US), because hygiene and peace of mind. You know what I love? Clean floors. I can't make everyone in my house maintain a shoeless household at all times, but once every few weeks or months, both the living room and hallway carpets are vacuumed and the kitchen is mopped. Then. *Then.* A breath so large and calming fills my body, and for once—for five minutes!—I can walk through my house in bare feet, like in a motherfucking Swiffer commercial, without getting grit on the bottoms of my feet.

Then someone tromps in from the backyard in their shoes or pees in their pajamas or eats crackers without a fucking plate.

Overall, cleaning makes me angry. If I'm cleaning something, I'm probably angry, because it means I've been staring at it for days, hoping someone else will clean it, and by the time I finally break down and just do it myself, I'm enraged. Tidying runs a close second. I spend 95 percent of my time putting things away, and guess what? They're not my things!

I have a bitter, ongoing fantasy that a research team follows SJ and me around our house, watching us and logging everything we do, so that, once and for all, I have hard data on what I already know: I DO MORE HOUSEWORK.

I've tried charts and chore wheels. FAIL. The labor it takes to put together a chart is one thing. But the labor of reminding the other person what week in the rotation it is, watching with mounting anxiety as the week sails by without said chores being done, and then nagging after the fact so said person will complete said chores while the week switches over and next week's chores mount up? TOO MUCH.

I've tried positive reinforcement. I've tried asking in "the right tone of voice." I've tried scathing personal attacks. Nothing works.

So, I make lists.

Here are some things SJ will not do under any circumstances:

- Anything that has to do with our son's clothing.

- Put away the clean dishes from the drain board.

- Clean out the fridge.

- Dust.

- Wipe down surfaces.

- Put his dishes in the dishwasher.

- Clean the kitchen sink.

- Wash bedclothes.

- Vacuum under the beds.

- Wash a window.

- Wipe a wall or any other high-touch, grimy area like a light switch, the edge of a door, or a cabinet.

- Take out the garbage and recycling if it's overflowing if it's not the night before it's collected.

- Empty the bathroom and bedroom garbage bins.

- Any kind of between-deep-cleanings upkeep of the bathroom.

- Walk past a clean surface without putting something on it.

- Give the dog water.

- Clean a rug.

- Put something away.

Here are some things SJ will do if I ask him to:

- Vacuum and sweep.

- Clean the bathroom.

- Mop the kitchen floor.

- Take out the compost.

Here are some things SJ will sometimes do on his own:

- Make a grocery list.

- Unload the dishwasher BUT ONLY IF THINGS ARE REALLY BAD.

- Sweep the kitchen floor.

Here is what SJ will do if he wants to have sex:

- Clean the top of the stove.

Here are some things SJ will do willingly and without being asked:

- Grocery shop.

- Pick up dog poop from the back yard.

- Sweep the front steps and driveway free of leaves from the coast live oak he had planted in the sidewalk square in front of our house and that drops leaves and acorns year-round.

- Take out the garbage and recycling the night before it's collected.

- Feed the dog.

- Pick up multipart kids' toys.

Here are some things SJ will do instead of cleaning:

- Buy a coconut from Grocery Outlet for the express purpose of trying to cut it open with a machete in our backyard.

- Sit in the backyard with an agave leaf making "rope."

If you're in a committed relationship, and both people work, which can mean one person works at a job and the other does the child care, and the division of housework is not down the middle, you're either angry (the one doing more housework) or a horrible excuse for a person (the one doing less housework).

If you live with extended family, make sure you're picking up after yourself.

If you're a single parent, God help you.

Magazines and the internet will try to tell you that, through household cleaning hacks, there's an easier, more efficient, less time-consuming, more effective, happier way to clean.

THERE'S NOT. LET'S STOP WITH THE HACKS AND FOCUS ON EQUITABLE DIVISION OF LABOR.

THEIR HACKS

- CLEAN YOUR SILVERWARE WITH BAKING SODA (an actual headline)

NO.

JENNY TRUE'S HACKS FOR KEEPING A CLEAN HOME WHILE RAISING A CHILD

- 9 Places to Check for Dust and Then Go Back to What You Were Doing Earlier

- Baseboards: Who Cares?

- 8 Vacuum Cleaner Extensions You Will Never Use But Never Throw Away

- 6 Dustpans with Cute Designs That Won't Affect How You Feel About Sweeping

- 7 Art Supplies Your Home Can Prove Are Not "Washable"

- 41 Better Uses of Your Time Than Cleaning Out the Fridge

- 5 Reasons Fruit Flies Are Not That Big of a Deal

37) **fuck laundry**
You do it.

For the last three years, I've been keeping track of how often SJ has contributed to the mountain of responsibilities known as "clothing." My notes show me this is his sole contribution: Once, he went to a party I didn't go to. Another mom—one of *his* friends—had arranged with *me* to meet him at the party with bags of hand-me-downs. When SJ got home, he parked the van in the garage and came upstairs.

"Where are the clothes?" I asked.

"In the van," he said, feet up on the couch, playing Tetris on his phone.

When it comes to kids' clothing, it's not just washing the clothes. It's acquiring them (getting donations from other people, shopping online or in stores), separating them, washing them, drying them, sorting them, folding them, putting them away, separating out the ones that have become too small, and getting rid of them: either donating them to other people (involves: sorting, packaging, arranging drop-offs or pickups, sometimes driving), donating to thrift stores (involves: sorting, packaging, sometimes driving), turning old clothes into rags or recycling them or storing the ones you want to keep so you can occasionally stare at them and cry or, if you really have time, taking them to consignment stores on the off chance you can resell something, either for cash or in-store credit.

For what it's worth, I don't do another adult's laundry. I established this with boyfriends when I was in high school (because when I was in high school in Quincy, Illinois, girls in high school washed their boyfriends' laundry, especially if their boyfriends went to the local college and were on the college football team). When it comes to household duties, laundry is the easiest task to separate out: SJ has his own laundry basket, and if he wants clean clothes, I have zero to do with it.

However, SJ has a habit of doing what he calls "Laund," wherein he puts a load of his laundry in the washer but leaves it there for days, or puts a load in the dryer but doesn't turn it on, so him doing his own laundry does not absolve me from doing *work*: I often need to move his laundry from the washing machine into the dryer to access the washing machine, and then move it from the dryer to the top of the dryer to access the dryer,

and every once in a while I'll just fucking fold it, because if I go so far as to transport his dry laundry from the top of the dryer to the sofa (unfolded), I will lose the opportunity to sit on the sofa for a few weeks; if I transfer it to the bed, he will happily sleep beside it, like a clean, lumpy lover, and pick clean clothes out of it as he needs them; and if I dump it on the floor, I leave myself open to criticism for being passive-aggressive (not untrue).

I could, at any point, remind him, or ask him, to finish his fucking laundry, but this is what is known as *mental load*, which we'll get to in chapter 39.

Remember when I said I don't do another adult's laundry? I should have said I don't do another adult's laundry *willingly* or *while smiling*. However, I do it silently, seething with rage, quoting Gloria Steinem. Also, any money I find is mine.

"There's also the chore of sorting, labeling, and storing clothes so the next child has hand-me-downs. In my mind, my husband doesn't appreciate this task enough or thank me enough for all the money we save. He mildly complains about bringing bins up and down from the basement once one of the boys has outgrown their size or when the seasons change." —JASMINE, mom of two

THEIR HACKS

- HOW TO MAKE A LAUNDRY SOAP DISPENSER
  (an actual headline)

NOT A HACK. MORE WORK.

JENNY TRUE'S HACKS FOR KEEPING UP WITH LAUNDRY WHILE RAISING A CHILD

- 3 Shirts without Armpits You Need Now

- The No. 1 Laundry "Accident" That Will Ensure You'll Never Be Allowed to Do Laundry Again (Hint: It Involves Bleach)

- 6 Common Reactions to the Term *Dry Clean Only*

- 25 Alternate Uses for an Iron

- 25 Alternate Uses for an Ironing Board

- Clean Clothes: Your Kid Doesn't Care, So Why Should You?

38) division of labor, work/life balance, and sasquatch
Myths that won't die.

I spend a lot of time complaining about the uneven distribution of household chores in my home. I'm a feminist, and my credentials are solid: I interned at *Ms.* magazine in 1997. I'm fluent in the language of *The Second Shift* by Arlie Hochschild. When the CEO of my nonprofit called me "dear," instead of smiling and imploding, I said, "Don't call me dear." (Years later, when he caught himself calling me "dear" again, he corrected himself. That time I smiled.)

But last year, when I found a dead rat in the garage, SJ and I somehow agreed it was his job to clean it up. I must have run over it with my car, either once or twice, but the question of how it got under my tire is a mystery. Rats are speedy, and I pull into the garage slowly, so it's not like I surprised it. So that leaves the rat being dead already in the path of my tire, but how did it die? We don't have rat traps out in the open, so did it have a heart attack on its way across the floor? Did it fall from the ceiling? If so, how did a low fall kill it? Etcetera.

Anyway, normally we find desiccated rats that have been caught by traps or that have died behind a box or something, and although they're not pleasant, they're not exactly gross because they don't look like rats anymore.

SJ (inquiring about the dead rat): Is it flat?
JENNY: No. That's why it's gross.

Jancee Dunn, who wrote the postpartum bible *How Not to Hate Your Husband after Kids*, calls household and child-care chores "donkeywork," and I will never, ever call them anything else again.

But sometimes I wonder if I shoulder most of the donkeywork because (1) I want chores done my way, and (2) there are certain other things I don't want to deal with. To wit:

- **Pipes**
- **Lighting the pilot light**
- **Installing things**
- **Fixing things**
- **Dead animals**

Division of labor varies depending on what kind of relationship you're in. Not in one? It's all you. In a heteronormative relationship? The female-type person is likely shouldering most, if not all, of the donkeywork. In a queer relationship? The chances of things being equitable get higher.

heteronormative

"My work/life balance has been me flying by the seat of my pants and praying it all gets done, which has become a reoccurring nightmare! This has led to a rise in stress level and the slow development of what I'm sure is an autoimmune disorder that doctors have yet to diagnose. Running a house with kids is a FULL-time business. And if BOTH partners aren't contributing to the day-to-day work, then the one shouldering everything is dying inside trying to work full-time or part-time, run all the evening activities, school the kids, shop, cook dinner, attend all the events—oh, yeah, and clean and keep the house and still have sex at night, which, after all that, you could care less about!"

—**DIANE**, *mom of two*

queer

"In our two-woman house, I'd say the division of labor is pretty darn equal. We do the things the other one hates. For instance, I clean out the dish drainer, and she folds clothes." —**CHRISSY**, mom of one

"I'm extra super-sparkly lucky: I have a partner who really does shoulder his share of parenting, running a household, and doing the work needed to maintain interpersonal connections within and outside of the family, which is my handy definition of mental load. After my divorce from someone who managed to get mildew on a wooden cutting board, I found a guy who LIKES SCRUBBING THE BATHTUB. He also does windows. I'm keeping him." —**LORI**, mom of two

your friendly hetero neighbors up the street who defy gender norms

"Any parent of a kid with special needs will tell you that the extra work that goes into getting services for your kid can be a lot. Our daughter has OT, speech, psychiatry, neurology, endocrinology, genetics, orthodontics, and developmental-pediatrics therapy . . . in addition to the usual doctor, dentist, teacher conferences, ballet stuff. It all gets divided up and often doesn't feel like there's enough of either of us. I'm blessed because my husband does a LOT of cleaning, and he's blessed because I love to cook. We meet weekly on Sunday nights to calendar and spend time together, and then often to drink wine and watch a K-drama." —**ANN**, mom of two

THE JENNY TRUE QUIZ ABOUT HOW MUCH YOUR LIFE SUCKS

1 I am in a:

- ○ *Heteronormative partnership*
- ○ *Same-sex partnership*
- ○ *Mixed-gender partnership*
- ○ *Polyamorous relationship*
- ○ *I'm single.*

2 I do most of the housework (more than 50 percent):

- ○ *True*
- ○ *False*

3 I do most of the child care (more than 50 percent):

- ○ *True*
- ○ *False*

4 I work for pay:

- ○ *Part-time (less than 40 hours a week)*
- ○ *Full-time (40 hours or more a week)*
- ○ *Seasonally/Sporadically*

5 I have a chronic health condition that is exacerbated by stress:

- ○ *True*
- ○ *False*

6 How does this quiz make you feel so far?

- ○ *Self-satisfied with my life and my choices!*
- ○ *A light is slowly dawning. Why am I the one who always makes the beds?*
- ○ *Filled with a boiling rage.*

7 Do you enjoy doing donkeywork?

- ○ *Yes*
- ○ *No*

8 Do you have any ideas the rest of us haven't thought of about how to effect a global change in the division of household labor?

- ○ *Yes. I'll DM you.*
- ○ *No. The game is rigged! There's no hope! Take your pleasure where you can!*

9 What do you think when you hear the term *work/life balance*?

- ○ *Hahahaha.* —**JANET,** *mom of two*
- ○ *Huh?* —**KRISTEN,** *mom of two*
- ○ *Let me know if you find it.* —**DIANE,** *mom of two*

39) **mental load**

A breakdown (so you can have a breakdown).

When I was a sophomore in college, my mother announced that we would not be having a Christmas tree that year.

"*You* can have one," she told us. "But I don't want to deal with it. You get it, you decorate it, you take it down, and you vacuum."

Then she spent the next week in a corner of the couch, reading a novel.

At the time, this seemed like a crime of the highest degree. Christmas meant tradition—we'd always had a tree! And it meant togetherness, even more important now that I was away at school (my brother often reminds me darkly, "It was only me at home for two years. YOU DON'T KNOW WHAT IT WAS LIKE WITH THEM").

How could my mother destroy our family tradition with one self-serving move?

Now I fucking get it.

I am the one in my family who remembers things. I remind people of things or silently implode as I don't remind them and watch appointments get missed, flutes get forgotten, tasks go undone. I am the main contact for the pediatrician and the day care. I keep the household budget and control the savings accounts. I manage the health care and the AAA membership. I am the one who notices and sees through to completion the tasks other people do half-assed—turning the dishwasher on once someone else has put the soap in and walked away, transferring day-old wet laundry from the washer to the dryer, wiping down the kitchen table once someone else has "cleared" it, putting out the salt and pepper and getting everyone water once someone else has "set the table." I buy things we're low on instead of waiting until we're completely out and fucked without them. I create charts for the refrigerator and calendars online and lists on whiteboards no one else uses or references. I know where everything in the bathroom and kitchen and bedrooms and living room and garage is (admittedly because I put everything where I think it should be, not necessarily where it's been for the past five years).

"Mental load" is the work that goes beyond the simple doing of chores: It's the invisible labor of managing a household, and it will kill me, and you, unless we kill everyone else first.

Note: This fun feature of many heteronormative relationships is not as bad in other kinds of relationships. (And if you're not partnered, you don't have to deal with it at all. But you have to do everything yourself!)

"Everything from planning their meals, to their social/learning development, their health/hygiene, their sleep habits/schedule, their schooling, their medical appointments, etc., takes an absurd amount of psychological real estate."

—**KRISTEN,** *mom of two*

This is what the unseen labor of the mental load is made up of (Hint: It's almost completely MENTAL):

- Managing
- Remembering
- Organizing
- List-making
- Scheduling
- Planning

- Following up
- Researching
- Deciding
- Choosing
- Asking
- Reminding

- Keeping track
- Negotiating
- Pleading
- Fuming
- Crying

the jenny true quiz:

WHAT WOULD YOU RATHER DO?

1

○ Keep track of the hundreds of vaccinations my kid is required to have.

○ Drink a paloma in a lawn chair.

2

○ Ask my partner to put his fucking dishes in the dishwasher.

○ Explore an ice cave near Jökulsárlón in southern Iceland.

3

○ Constantly do math to see how long we could all eat if I got laid off from my job.

○ Try on sunglasses at Nordstrom Rack.

4

○ Research day cares and do interviews on the phone and arrange for in-person interviews and come up with questions and ask the questions and keep track of the answers to compare with other day cares later.

○ Vacation in Ibiza with celebrity-adjacent people.

5

O Realize it's time to start childproofing and then do an audit of our house to see what needs to be child-proofed and then research products online and then order them and then either install them myself or make sure they get installed.

O Hold a very soft bunny.

6

O Make sure my partner transfers the AAA membership card I handed him into his wallet so it's not on my desk the next time his twenty-year-old minivan that needs a new battery won't start.

O Drink an iced, sweetened cold brew at a roadside stand in Hanalei, Kauai.

7

O Coordinate calendars with my partner to make a well-baby appointment with the pediatrician and hunt him down to fill out the question-naire together about which milestones our son has or has not reached, then go to said appointment alone when my partner schedules a work meeting at the same time.

O Climb the Torre del Mangia in Siena, Italy, and then eat seafood salad and drink a Vernaccia in the Piazza del Campo.

(continued)

8

○ *Politely request that "cleaning up" after dinner not mean leaving the dirty dishes and pots and pans on the table and the counters and in the sink for twenty-four hours until five minutes before the next dinner is being prepared.*

○ *Scuba-dive on a coral reef in Pulau Menjangan, Indonesia.*

9

○ *Research pediatricians when our initial pediatrician, who is twenty-four, decides to quit her job and travel the world with her husband, because they are young and don't have children and can do things like quit their jobs and travel the world like I used to do.*

○ *Go to a movie theater with a tallboy wrapped in a yoga mat and sit in the dark, alone, tippling and watching a film about a middle-aged woman with ennui, who worries that something's wrong, but in the end nothing is wrong (SJ claims this is my favorite genre).*

10

○ *Research streaming services with kids' programming so our son can watch Frozen and Cars as many times as he fucking wants and at any time.*

○ *Write and publish a mass-market book that calls out my partner on the unequal division of labor in our home, MY FANTASY-MADE MANIFEST.*

the jenny true worksheet:

FOR THE NEW PARENT WHO HAS LOCKED THEMSELF IN THE BATHROOM WITH THEIR PHONE AND A GLASS OF WINE (AGAIN)

1 The thing I most regret about having a child:

_____

_____

2 My body used to resemble:

_____

_____

3 Now it resembles (get creative!):

_____

_____

4 My breasts used to resemble:

_____

_____

5 Now they resemble (get creative!):

_____

_____

(continued)

6 On Sunday mornings I used to:

_____

_____

7 I used to have sex _____ times a day/week/month.

8 Before having a child, I had pooped in front of someone else _____ times in my life.

9 Before having a child, I was vomited on _____ times in my life.

10 Rate the following in order of importance:

_____ *Seven to nine hours of continuous sleep*

_____ *Five fucking minutes to myself*

_____ *A single bowel movement without a child pounding on the door*

_____ *An afternoon to sit in a coffee shop during the day eating a doughnut and staring out the window at NOTHING. NOTHING.*

11 My girlfriend/boyfriend from high school's phone number is:

_____

12 It wouldn't be weird to text them out of the blue and ask what they've been up to:
- ○ *True*
- ○ *False*

13 These are the people who would know I'm just being friendly because I'm a friendly person:

a. _____

14 These are the people who would interpret this as a cry for help:

a. _____

b. _____

c. _____

d. _____

e. _____

15 If I never come out of this room, my child/children will still grow up to be healthy, happy, and functional:

O *True*

O *False*

O *That was never going to happen anyway.*

16 This bathroom smells like dirty towels and I'm just realizing that the toilet hasn't been flushed.

O *GODDAMMIT*

17 I deserve five minutes to myself:

O *True*

O *PLEASE GOD MAKE IT TEN*

EPILOGUE
forget everything you just read

HAVING A BABY IS THE BEST THING EVER!

After I had a baby, my life got very, very narrow. Whereas before I had a wide social circle and often engaged in "activities," such as "social outings" and "exercise," now I spent large chunks of time doing what previously looked like doing nothing: lying in bed, sitting in a patio chair, sitting in a swing, all holding my baby. And I LOVED IT. After more than forty years of closing down the bars, you finally realize that NOTHING INTERESTING HAPPENS AFTER ABOUT 11 P.M.

No matter what I write to get a laugh, and no matter what is true about my anxiety and the difficulties of pregnancy and parenting, being the mother to my child has given purpose to my life. Nothing makes me happier. NOTHING. I AM SO FUCKING HAPPY. I miss my son when I'm not with him, including when he's asleep. I can't believe he's so cute and funny. I'm grateful for how I've had to slow my life down, and narrow it to the essentials, to accommodate him. I am constantly amazed at the world, and it's the same world I lived in before he was born. Holding him and kissing him are my favorite things. I don't know what the fuck I was doing before.

I do not believe that no one else in the universe has known love like this, the way I once believed no one else had ever been so sad, or aggrieved, or in love. Instead I believe that these intense, unrelenting, complex, overwhelming feelings are the least unique of all, and this gives me a deeper understanding of and compassion for our world and less fear of speaking out.

I smile when I think of my kid. I think about my kid to make myself smile.

"I would say that some moments—even simple ones, like when my daughter's dozing off to sleep after a fight and instead of showing me her back, her hand reaches for my wrist—fill me with a forceful, intense love that I only knew shades of before becoming a parent. Lately I've been watching my son do his ballet exercises on Zoom with defined muscles on display, come up with a berry sauce for the dark chocolate soufflés he has baked for my birthday, and quietly take my hand as we walk around the garden, and I'm filled with this same love tinged with pride and wonder that I get to be part of this marvelous life."

—**ANN**, *mom of two*

"It terrifies me how much I love them. Loving them is my greatest vulnerability. My love feels like a tidal wave that could consume this whole goddamn house. My love feels like all my emotions tightly bottled into the single experience of being their mother. And that kinda feels like the point—for it to devastate and reward.

"I am captivated by their every expression, not wanting to miss a millisecond. Then I am overwhelmed with grief at how fleeting it all is. I already miss them as babies, toddlers, elementary school students, teenagers, grown men with their own lives. I devote myself each day to love and develop them into functional men who will eventually leave me. Even as I manage my impending loss, I understand that it is a privilege and honor to have lived. I hope when my time comes to let them go, it will be those experiences that comfort me."

—KRISTEN, *mom of two*

"Me before baby: Side-eyeing all the moms and grandmas saying things like, 'I want to gobble them up,' and pretending to munch on the babies' toes. WTF? Why is everyone always talking about eating their children?

"I now understand that there is no way to accurately describe this all-consuming love that leaves you wishing you could soak up this perfect little being until you've fully absorbed them and enveloped them in your adoration and protection.

"Me after baby: Constantly looking for new, creative ways to explain to my baby which body part I'm about to ingest."

—ALLISON, *mom of one*

"The beginning of our family was wrought with trying times. We had to cope with the deaths of three parents in eleven months, while having a toddler and a baby in a sling two thousand miles from the nearest person we could count on, new jobs, new cities, and multiple moves. But I find myself wishing I could go back to the baby years. It wasn't true insanity. It was learning how to cope with huge life changes.

"We have been blessed to spend a lot of time with our kids. This is not how we were raised. It's just what felt right for us. Now that they're teenagers, I joke that if my daughter could, she'd still hang out in a sling on my hip. They are fun. They are creative. They are unique. They crack me up. I really do enjoy every minute of it."

—DIANE, *mom of two*

"When my daughter was three, I was putting her to bed, knowing she was going to ask for water, get up to say one more goodnight, call out again. I was bracing for that drown-out irritation that just pulled at my exhaustion like taffy, when she took my face in her hands and said, 'I want to dream about you, Mommy.' I could feel myself stretch and deepen like a pillow pushing into every fold, just like I've felt continuously since the day she was born." —CHRISSY, mom of one

"Being this kid's mom has opened the door to heal my own childhood trauma and learn how to be more kind, gentle, and patient. I am in awe at how resilient our relationship is. Even on the worst days, when mom rage takes over, I can always muster an apology, or he'll run to me and say, 'Mommy, I have something to tell you. I love you.' My heart melts all over, and I'm reminded that my daily lesson is to just stay present and grounded." —STEPHANIE, mom of one

"There are parts of me that I don't remember before having kids. Like what I like to do with my free time, like sleep, veg out on social media, or try to sneak-watch non-kid-friendly shows with my husband. But having kids has also shown me more of who I am. I have a capacity for selflessness, tenderness, and a passion to fight for a world that's better for all kids that I don't think I would have tapped into without being a mother.

"I breastfed my second son for eighteen months. He's three now and still insists on hugging me multiple times a day with his hand in my shirt, right over my heart like he did when he was nursing. For a split second, I feel guilty because I think, 'Maybe I cut him off too soon,' but then I just melt into his embrace and thank God for our special bond." —JASMINE, mom of two

"I still weep when I think about looking at her for the first time. I love her in my bones, with my whole heart and every atom that makes me. At its most mundane, my love for her feels like that first sip of caffeine and a bite of warm toast. At its most intense, it feels like a tsunami, crashing tidal waves of joy into my mainland brain.

"It took so much to get my child into the world, and I am so much better as a person because of her. She is all that's good and untainted. I feel fortunate that she thinks I'm cool enough to be her friend. I love every aspect of helping her navigate the world, even when she's kicking me or throwing up in my mouth. Having a kid that's mine, like half me, is just surreal and incredible."

—DONNIE, *dad of one*

"Earlier this week, I was on Zoom calls all day long, with no lunch break until deep in the afternoon. I let my kids know, just so they understood I was going to be unable to respond to minor incidents and they were on their own for lunch. Completely unsolicited, one kid made me a peanut butter and jelly sandwich and silently slid it onto my desk, out of range of my laptop camera, so I could eat lunch 'with' them.

"Not long after, my diabetic partner came home from a long day of work and let me know his blood sugar was low. My other kid overheard and rushed to the pantry, grabbed a lollipop, and ran to offer it to him.

"I seem to have managed to raise two thoughtful, loving kids who look after themselves, each other, and their friends and family. I really want to take All The Credit for this, except I'm not sure what I did! But I hope their thoughtfulness and compassion extends to the rest of the people in their lives in the future, and that it's properly reciprocated, because they deserve all the love."

—LORI, *mom of two*

acknowledgments

As with children, this book, written entirely during the coronavirus pandemic, would not have been possible without a village.

Thank you to my agent, Laura Lee Mattingly, for taking a chance on parenting humor. Seeing your name in my inbox brings me joy.

Thank you to my excellent editor at Running Press, Jennifer Kasius, for making my dreams come true. Every time you told me I was funny, a neurosis withered and died. I'm sorry I tried to put a picture of a tube of Preparation-H on the cover (but I can't promise I won't do it again!).

Thank you to Katina Papson-Rigby and Jasmine Hood Miller, two excellent readers, mamas, and friends who provided thoughtful, incisive, and generous feedback. Thank you to Kristianna Gehant, my column reader and friend for thirty years.

Thank you to my fellow parents for sharing their stories and allowing me to use them here: Jill Alexander, Sasha Clayton, Amanda Davidson, Chrissy Elgersma, Cati Brown Johnson, Ann Kim, Allison Frost Macari, Kristen Ohiaeri, Janet Manley, Jasmine Hood Miller, Stephanie Ong, Katina Papson-Rigby, Robin Romm, Isaac Schankler, Lori Selke, Jessica Slice, and Donnie Weaver.

For early illustrations and inspiration, thank you to brilliant cartoonist Amanda Davidson. For excellent medical-type feedback and research help, thank you to Karen Meyer, CNM. For insight into her experience in the doula community, thank you to Emily Pulstus.

Thank you to Janet Manley for plucking me out of obscurity to write an advice column. But mostly, thank you for inspiring me with your vast knowledge, multiple talents, fortitude, and humor. None of this would have happened without you. Special thanks to April Daniels Hussar and Margaret Wheeler Johnson at Romper for consistently supporting the "Dear Jenny" column and all things Jenny True.

Thank you to Wren Brennan for naming the book. Thank you to Abigail Martin Del Campo Muñoz for email marketing advice and Spanish lessons. Thank you to Ellen Seebold for showing me how to use Instagram. Thank you to Paolo Asuncion and Jenn Keys for multiple photo shoots, gorgeous pictures, and friendship to our family. Thank you to Claire Seizovic for a website redesign and brand guidance I'M A BRAND NOW IT'S WHAT I'VE ALWAYS WANTED MWAHAHAHA, and thank you to Arne Johnson, Kristen Ohiaeri, and Shane King for the hilarious Jenny True videos WHAT YOU HAVEN'T SEEN THEM GO TO MY WEBSITE.

Thank you to famous poet Julie Bruck, who sent me to Lenka Clayton's Artist Residency in Motherhood, which started me on this project. Thank you to artist and mama Lenka Clayton. I love everything you do and would like to tell you in person one day. Thank you to Jane Friedman for excellent and affordable online courses on writing and book publishing.

A note on friends: I was afraid to get started here in case I left anyone out, but if I'm not creating a situation that will pain me in the future, am I really me? Friendship makes life possible. Some of the following people take care of my son, some read my horrible first drafts, some are my therapist, some call me to tell me things they really shouldn't because it's not our business but REALLY TELL ME, some text me "Moon!!!" when it's a full moon so I won't miss it, and all are supportive, consistent, present, positive, and real. Thank you to Leticia Ornelas, Esteban Gutiérrez, and Danica Gutiérrez of Manos de Angel Day Care in San Francisco. Thank you to Kathy Gilbert, Kaila Rain Thomas, Dina Saba, Lindsey Wolkin, Monica Wesolowska, Julie Fellom, Jessa Post, Brendan and Rachel Jones, Caroline Knorr, Angie Zimmerman, Kara Swedlow, Kirstin Dau, Rachel Smith, Andy and Jeana Peterson, Audrey Howard, Seth Macari and Allison Frost Macari, Agnes Szelag, Amanda Rusk, Kate Leahy, Derek Ellis, Gwen Warnock, Ernest Frohm, Janice Taylor, and Thad and Michiko Fowler.

Thank you, Mom and Dad. I was just kidding when I said you fucked me up (chapter 27). Isn't it nice we can joke this way? But seriously: You taught me to be loving and unafraid, a balance I work on every day.

Thank you to my brother, Jesse. Mostly for marrying Agua, the funniest person on the planet. I'm OK with the fact that we look exactly the same but somehow you're good-looking and I'm not. Meranti forever!

Thank you to my sister-in-law Agua for being the one thing our entire family can agree on.

Thank you, Tallulah. You are the best stepdaughter I could have hoped for: exuberant and independent and self-confident and funny and kind. My favorite thing is when we're all together in the van or at an airport or at urgent care. You blow my mind with how great a big sister you are. Thank you for putting up with me as I fail in ways I never anticipated.

Thank you to all my parents-in-law for raising a good human. I like you independently and would hang out with you even if I weren't married to Shane. Thank you to my sister-in-law Linea, for teaching me about resilience. You make retirement look good.

Thank you to Copper. I wrote the rest of the book about you, so I'm not going to go into it here. I mean, the book is *dedicated* to you. What more do you want?

Finally, thank you to Shane. It's really too bad that a book about your good qualities wouldn't sell. You are patient to a fault (obviously), and your commitment to social justice, family, and the earth are why our roots are entangled. I can't believe how much we make each other laugh. The hard times don't make me panic. I love you so much.

Ten percent of the advance for this book was donated to Sister-Song: Women of Color Reproductive Justice Collective. Listen to Black and Indigenous birthing people. Black lives matter.

about the author

Jenny True is Jenny Pritchett, a longtime writer and editor and nationally recognized columnist for Romper. Jenny's debut collection, *At or Near the Surface*, won the Michael Rubin Book Award. She has published fiction in *Boulevard*, the *Northwest Review*, the *Southwest Review*, *Salt Hill*, and other journals and has written and reported for Guernica, Salon, and *Bitch*, among others. Her work has been anthologized and selected for publication by Steve Almond and Michelle Richmond, and she has received fellowships from the Ragdale Foundation and the Tomales Bay Writing by Writers Workshop, a grant from San Francisco State University, and a scholarship from the Squaw Valley Community of Writers. Her story "Thieves" was nominated for a Pushcart Prize by the *Southwest Review*.

Jenny has a bachelor's degree from Northwestern University's Medill School of Journalism and an MFA in creative writing from San Francisco State University. She has taught creative writing at the Bay Area's Writing Salon since 2009 and at San Francisco State University and the Institute of American Indian Arts in Santa Fe, New Mexico. In a former life she was a fact-checker for *Sunset* and *Dwell* and an intern for *Mother Jones* and *Ms.*

As Jenny True, the voice of her blog and the "Dear Jenny" column, she has been recognized on the sidewalk by a mom driving by in a car, and a mom on a plane.

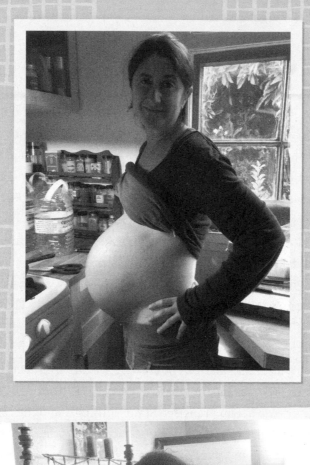

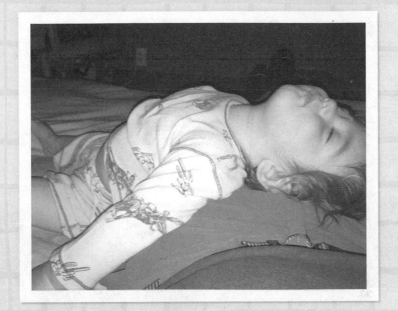

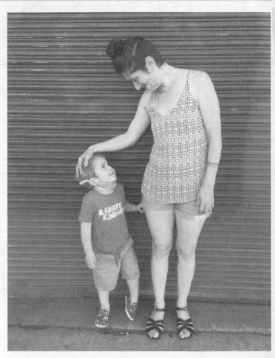